FROM BURNOUT
TO BALANCE

FROM BURNOUT TO BALANCE

A Workbook for
Peak Performance
and Self-Renewal

DENNIS T. JAFFE, Ph.D.,
and CYNTHIA D. SCOTT, Ph.D.

McGraw-Hill Book Company

New York St. Louis San Francisco Bogotá Guatemala Hamburg Lisbon Madrid
Mexico Montreal Panama Paris San Juan São Paulo Tokyo Toronto

First McGraw-Hill Paperback edition, 1984

1 2 3 4 5 6 7 8 9 SEM SEM 8 7 6 5 4

ISBN 0-07-032186-8

Library of Congress Cataloging in Publication Data

Jaffe, Dennis T.
From burnout to balance.
Bibliography: p.
Includes index.
1. Burn-out (Psychology)—Prevention. 2. Mental health. I. Scott, Cynthia D. II. Title.
BF482.J34 1984   158'.1   84-4395
ISBN 0-07-032186-8 (pbk.)

BOOK DESIGN BY PATRICE FODERO

To the pioneers of health promotion, the creators of the revolution in health care—who include researchers, practitioners, and enlightened consumers

ACKNOWLEDGMENTS

This book is a synthesis of what we have learned in the past decade from the work of important researchers, theorists, and clinicians in the fields of health and humanistic psychotherapy. Most of these people are unaware of their contribution to our work, but we would like to acknowledge our debt to them: Aaron Antonovsky, Herbert Benson, David Burns, Rick Carlson, Norman Cousins, Ken Dychtwald, Albert Ellis, Tom Ferguson, Herbert Freudenberger, Meyer Friedman, Charles Garfield, David Glass, Willis Goldbeck, Thomas Holmes, C. D. Jenkins, Ari Kiev, Suzanne Kobasa, Richard Lazarus, Emmett Miller, Rudolph Moos, Ken Pelletier, Ayala Pines, Richard Rahe, Naomi Remen, Ray Rosenman, Gary Schwartz, Richard Seligman, Gabriel Smilkstein, Shelley Taylor, and John Travis. We thank them for doing the research, which we hope we are making available to a wider audience.

We would also like to thank the Robert Simon Foundation for providing a grant to the Center for Integral Medicine, which helped support the gathering of material for this book.

CONTENTS

CHAPTER 1

Self-Management in a World of Stress

The working person of yesterday was most likely concerned with direct production. He or she worked on the farm, at home, or in a shop or factory. Today the majority of workers are concerned with information and service. People work with customers, or clients, transferring information, preparing reports, and often interacting intensely with each other. This new environment demands vast new sets of skills. Instead of physical stamina and routine tasks, we are today presented with multiple demands, many choices and decisions, and a world in which we need to work together on complex tasks. Instead of physical activity, the primary demands are mental and interpersonal.

At work and in personal and family life many people find themselves feeling overwhelmed and struggling to get things under control. They feel pressured by time and continually need to respond and act, often without having a clear idea of the outcome. Life is made up of pressures and uncertainty, to which we need to adapt.

People respond to the modern world with a body and a mind that were designed to function well in a far simpler world. Our primary mental and physical characteristics evolved several million years ago, whereas the world we inhabit today was created by us not even a generation ago. The things that we demand of ourselves are not the things that we were designed to do. As a result, we fall prey to all manner of physical and emotional forms of illness and distress, and we experience difficulty and distress with the life we lead. At an extreme many people have begun to use the term "burnout" to refer to a generalized depletion of energy, lack of involvement, and inability to function well and achieve satisfaction. Many people feel burned out and helpless to do anything to overcome it.

There must be a better way, we think to ourselves. How can we cope with the pressures of our work and our lives? Is it possible to preserve ourselves from illness and distress? How can we perform our jobs effectively and meet the demands upon us?

Effective coping requires that we develop a new view of ourselves and a new set of skills and awarenesses. In the traditional view the person was primarily reactive, responding reflexively and automatically to pressures and demands. The person was primarily determined by the circumstances of his or her life, and in order to live well had merely to continue offering the correct responses to the environment, which was also predictable and regular. Today the environment has been changed, and we need to respond by changing ourselves.

The new, emerging view of the person begins with the observation that in addition to reacting to pressures and demands, we have the ability to modify ourselves and respond to demands in creative and novel ways. The human being, unlike a machine or most other forms of life, can reorganize in response to pressure and change. Thus, when pressures build up, instead of reacting to them one at a time, we also have the capacity to plan, to consider alternatives, and then to attempt something completely new and different. The new view of the person emphasizes the unique human ability to be creative, to adapt by reorganizing and redefining the situation, and to become self-determining. Instead of giving up or giving in to daily pressures, we can evolve and adapt.

Many people today seek some form of training in various aspects of life management. They attend seminars and read books about self-regulation techniques, life planning, time management, visualization and guided imagery, positive thinking, interpersonal skills, assertion, and conflict resolution. With this guidance people expect to learn how to overcome self-created pain and distress, master their lives, and realize their potentials. This vast array of workshops presents common themes and techniques. They all emphasize increasing self-awareness, taking responsibility for life choices, clarifying needs and intentions in situations, increasing personal risks, modifying self-defeating patterns of thought and action, and actively responding to demands.

The central message of this book is that in our complex and demanding world people need to learn how to manage, maintain, and renew themselves. These skills are as essential to self-preservation and effective work performance as the traditional skills of managing people and resources outside of oneself. Traditional management training and organizational practices have for too long neglected the needs of the individual and teaching people to be sensitive to themselves. As a result, signs and symptoms of burnout are epidemic. The skills presented in this book all center on helping the beleaguered worker to gain greater control and mastery over himself and his life situations, so that he will no longer feel victimized, overwhelmed, or attacked by pressures and demands. The authors show people how to increase their self-awareness and practice self-renewal, self-management, self-determination, and self-care.

This workbook is designed to help you respond creatively to the pressure and demands of your work and your life. The goal is not simply to keep you healthy and to avoid getting burned out from life stress, but also to help you perform up to your capacity to achieve your personal level of *peak performance*. You can learn those skills through a process of self-exploration. At each step of the way you will be looking at various aspects of your life and work, and assessing the effectiveness of your functioning. Then you will learn how to respond more creatively.

Learning new ways involves three types of activity. First you will have to look closely at what you are doing already and rethink those responses. You will have to ask yourself critically why you are doing certain things, and what effects these actions bring. This is *self-exploration* or *self-awareness*. The second type of activity is *self-renewal*, the inner exploration of the effects of your behavior on your body and your psyche, and the conscious regular attempts to rejuvenate and regenerate yourself. Under continual stress human beings need continual renewal. Finally, you will have to begin consciously to determine your strategies in response to daily pressures of work and personal life. You will have to practice the skills of *self-management*. This workbook teaches you the skills of self-management and self-renewal. The difference between self-management and reflex management of stress is the difference between a person who is in charge of his or her life, and a person whose life rules him or her. We all want to be in control of our destiny.

THE THREAT OF STRESS

A few decades ago if you asked anyone what causes disease, he or she would have answered, "germs." Today a more common answer would be stress. Stress is blamed for everything and is considered a necessary evil that we all need to live with. The truth, however, is that while stress may be involved in the creation of many modern forms of illness and distress, the stress response within our body is actually our primary protector, a mechanism that can be mobilized to preserve or to harm us. Stress can be our protector as well as our destroyer.

The word "stress" was coined in 1946 by Hans Selye, who spent his life looking at the general ways that the body protects itself against difficulty and danger. According to Selye, stress

> is the nonspecific response of the body to any demand placed upon it. . . . All agents and changes to which we are exposed produce a nonspecific increase in the need to perform adaptive functions and thereby to establish normalcy. . . . It is immaterial whether the agent or situation we face is pleasant or unpleasant; all that counts is the intensity of the demand for readjustment or adaptation.

The stress response is, thus, the response of our body to any change, demand, pressure, or threat from outside. The aim of the stress response is to bring the agitated or disturbed body back to normal and to enable it to protect itself from the external situation.

The demand to adapt comes from the continuing pressures of our work or our families and the internal pressures and demands we make on ourselves. The stress response is an ally whose aim is to keep us together physically and emotionally. Our lives are a continuing struggle against demands, which can spur us to creative achievements, provide us with excitement, or burn us out in bitterness, apathy, and frustration.

So how is it that the stress response in our body that is supposed to protect us, does us in? There are several reasons.

First, the sheer number of demands is often more than we can handle. We are assaulted by noise, cars, pollution, and the threat of crime or accident. The pace of change in our work and world is staggering; we continually need to respond to new situations. Today authors are writing books in a word processor, a machine that most people had never heard of until last year. At work executives are overloaded, pressured, or frustrated, and don't know how to respond. In personal relationships we don't feel we can get what we need from those around us, or we don't have someone to turn to for support.

The stress response is the emotional and psychological reaction that our body makes to each of these demands and changes. The body reacts the same way whether the demand is psychological—pressure to complete a job, conflict in a relationship—or physical—a car swerving at you, a mugger threatening you. No matter what the demand, our body mobilizes for physical action. However, most of the demands we face do not require quick, decisive physical action. Therefore, although the body is aroused for action many times a day, because the pressures are psychological, we inhibit our body's natural responses. This creates muscle tension, headaches, stomach cramps, and some of the more serious stress-related physical symptoms. Our body is poised for action, but our mind tells us to stop and stay put.

By not responding to demands physically, and by poor management of the work and other pressures, we keep ourselves in a continual state of physical arousal. The buildup is cumulative. The negative physical effects are due to inadequate, delayed, misplaced, or inhibited responses to pressure. Our body is never released, so tension builds up. Just like a car engine running when not in gear, or a toaster left on, our bodies burn out. In order to gain some control over this negative cycle, we need to cultivate the skills of self-awareness, self-renewal, and self-management.

All around us we can see people struggling ineffectively with stress, pressure, and tension. Smoking, drinking, drug use, and overeating are all ineffective responses to life stress. These form our major public health hazards and indirectly, in the form of accidents and impaired work performance, lead to inestimable harm and cost. The nation has perhaps 10 million alcoholics who cost around $43 billion per year in lost work time, insurance claims, and health and accident costs! People spend $3 billion on cigarettes and alcohol, but the nation and insurers pick up the tab for the resulting damage to health. Corporations lost $20 billion last year from absence and death due to smoking, and the direct costs were $8 billion. Each year there are over 150 million new prescriptions for moodaltering drugs, half of them for Valium and Librium.

There are short-term and long-term effects of our inability to manage stress effectively. Each day's frustrations, struggles, and difficulties lead to minor symptoms, pains, and emotional distress. These tensions cause distress, and we try a variety of effective and ineffective strategies to deal with them.

Over longer periods chronic daily stresses wear us down, causing more severe problems. As tension builds up, we may fruitlessly begin smoking, drinking, eating too much, or depending on some other form of addiction that carries with it its own negative effects, as well as poorly managing the long-term effects of stress. Many of our most severe health problems and social problems, ironically, stem from our own ineffective attempts to find relief from the tension of everyday stress. Serious illness can result from long-term stress or from self-defeating methods of managing it.

Emotional and psychological distress is also debilitating, and it takes an increasing human toll. The incidence of chronic depression and anxiety is rising, suggesting that these emotional states are one long-term result of daily stress. Marital difficulties, antisocial behavior, child and spouse abuse, and many forms of interpersonal conflict stem from inability to manage stress. And finally, the loss of meaning, commitment, and connection to work, family, or life tasks, which has been termed burnout, is increasing. It is as if daily stress is slowly using up people, leading to most of the serious social and health problems that our society faces.

The Effects of Stress

When people are under too much stress or they do not manage the stress they are under effectively, a wide variety of symptoms are experienced.

Physical effects: Elevated blood and urine catecholamines and corticosteroids; increased blood glucose, heart rate, and blood pressure; shallow, difficult breathing; numbness, tingling, and coldness in the extremities; queasy stomach; tight muscles; back and head pain; dry mouth and sweating. Over time these physical responses cause breakdown of vital organs, and serious and chronic disease.

Emotional effects: Anxiety, anger, boredom, depression, fatigue, frustration, irritability, moodiness, tension, nervousness, self-hate, worry.

Mental effects: Difficulty concentrating, poor task performance, defensiveness, focus on details, sleepiness, mental blocks.

Behavioral effects: Drug use, alcoholism, smoking, overeating, loss of appetite, impulsive or aggressive outbursts, accident proneness, restlessness, blaming others, withdrawal and isolation.

Organizational effects: Job burnout, low morale, absenteeism, poor performance, high turnover, job dissatisfaction, lawsuits, high use of health facilities, accidents, poor working relationships.

Excessive stress has negative effects on all dimensions of our life, creating physical, emotional, interpersonal, and organizational distress and damage.

THE STRESS CYCLE

In popular usage the word "stress" refers to the unpleasant feeling of pressure, excitement, or fatigue caused by demands, as well as to the demands that lead to this response. Thus stress refers to both the cause and the effect, suggesting that the two are so closely linked that it is hard to separate stimulus from response. This is important.

To clarify how the stress process takes place, it is necessary to outline the entire chain of events within us that produces it. Things can be done at each step that can reduce the negative or dysfunctional effects.

Stressors: The Trigger

All the external pressures, demands, threats, changes, conflicts, challenges, and difficulties we face can trigger our body's stress response. Anything that happens in our world that demands some change, adjustment, or response from us is termed a "stressor." In order to protect us, our body responds to almost anything. Indeed it errs on the side of caution, responding with alertness at the slightest hint something is wrong or that our reserves of energy will be needed.

Some of the most familiar stressors include:

* any life change or important life event
* threats to our person or self-esteem

- loss of someone or something we care for or depend on
- conflicting or ambiguous demands or expectations
- pressure of deadlines, too much work, and confused priorities
- conflict or difficulty with other people
- frustration or threats to our personal needs

Each individual finds some stressors more difficult or demanding than others; that has to do with our personal style and background. Everyone can list scores of common stressors in his or her daily life; most of us experience continual pressure in our lives. However, when we experience several pressures at once, or if a pressure is especially severe, our stress level increases and we are at risk of illness or personal crisis.

Evaluating the Threat

To a degree stress is manufactured within our minds. In order for our body to experience stress, our mind must consider a situation threatening or difficult. For example, two people may be given the same task. One person feels his job might be on the line, or has grave doubts about his ability. The other person, of the same ability and standing within the organization, might feel comfortable with herself and her job standing. The task would be perceived as more stressful by the first person.

People manufacture stress for themselves when they worry, anticipate the worst, or create unrealistic demands on themselves. When we imagine a stressful situation, our body acts as if the event is really happening and the stress response is triggered. Thus we can reduce stress simply by reducing the amount of negative thinking.

Several factors are important in determining how much stress we experience. First, our childhood learning creates patterns and expectations that we carry into adult life. Feelings about ourselves, our abilities, our expectations of ourselves and other people can all stem from childhood conditioning. Each person learns a style of responding to challenges and thinking about the world that greatly affects how safe or threatening the world appears to him or her. A person who feels safe and confident will experience less stress than one who is fearful and full of self-doubt.

The Stress Response

Regardless of the stressor and of the nature of our evaluation of it, when we perceive something as even mildly stressful, our entire body swings into immediate action. The muscles tighten, the brain sends signals to release adrenaline into the bloodstream, blood vessels constrict, the stomach tightens and secretes acid, breathing becomes quick and shallow, and we experience intense emotions such as rage, fear, anger, or anxiety. This integrated response to threat, which evolved eons ago to allow us to mobilize the tremendous energy needed for survival in a world of change and predators, can now be as much of a problem as a protector.

Many situations trigger unnecessary stress. We do not always need the physical arousal and mobilization of energy of this powerful reaction. Thus, for many situations, we need to learn to train ourselves either to avoid activating the stress response in the first place, or else, once activated, learn to turn it off. Otherwise we will literally burn ourselves out. The feelings of exhaustion, depletion, muscle tension, and depression are often signs that we have repeatedly aroused ourselves via the stress response with no release.

Turning Off

While there are many ways to turn on the stress response, there are relatively few methods to turn it off. Physically, we can turn off the response by taking direct, physical action against the situation or threat. Early in human evolution this meant fighting or fleeing; hence the term "fight/flight reaction" is often used for the first stage of the stress response. In most contemporary situations we can turn off the stress response by actively responding to a situation, or by physically exercising the stress out of our body. A third common method is through quiet forms of relaxation that activate an opposite response in the body, the relaxation response. Techniques such as meditation, progressive relaxation, guided imagery, biofeedback, and self-hypnosis can all activate this opposing psychophysiological state.

Tension: The Pathway to Illness and Distress

What we commonly refer to as stress is more properly labeled "tension." Tension is the buildup of unrelieved stress within our bodies. We experience tension as muscle tightness, aches and pains, upset stomach, anxiety or depression, feelings of depletion or lack of energy, emotional burnout, withdrawal and conflict in relationships. These symptoms crop up when we react repeatedly to stress and when we do not manage it effectively. Tension is the residue that is left when we feel we cannot do something about the stress we are under, when we fail to do something about it, or when we deny its existence and mask the signs of stress. Over time, tension signals that our body has worn down, and illness in the form of physical or emotional breakdown is the final result.

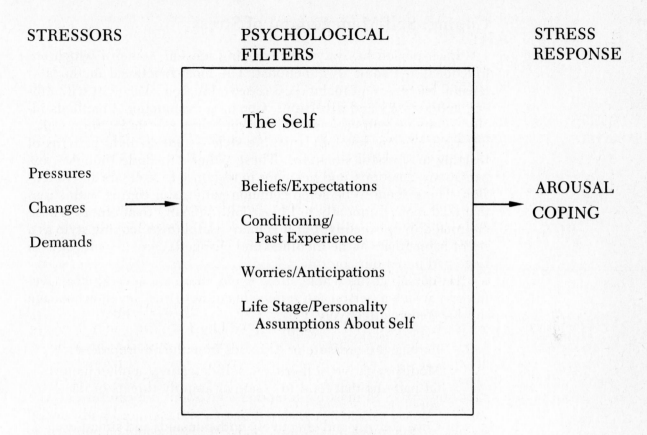

STRESSORS

Pressures

Changes

Demands

PSYCHOLOGICAL
FILTERS

The Self

Beliefs/Expectations

Conditioning/
   Past Experience

Worries/Anticipations

Life Stage/Personality
   Assumptions About Self

STRESS
RESPONSE

AROUSAL
COPING

Figure 1-1: TRIGGERING THE STRESS RESPONSE

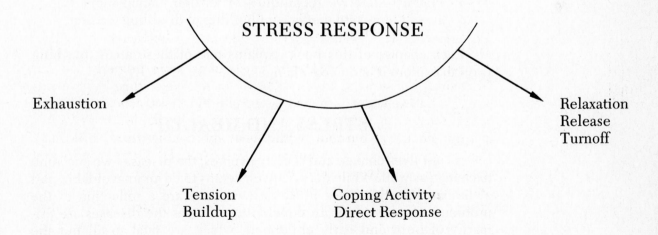

STRESS RESPONSE

Exhaustion

Tension
Buildup

Coping Activity
Direct Response

Relaxation
Release
Turnoff

Figure 1-2: OUTCOMES OF THE STRESS RESPONSE

Coping: Self-Management of Stress

Each person has ways of managing tension, some of which are functional and some dysfunctional. The most functional methods of tension management include exercise, relaxation, sharing it with others, and hobbies and diversions. Common dysfunctional methods include denying, eating, drinking, smoking, drug use, and withdrawal.

Each person develops a coping style—some general patterns of reacting to stressful situations. These patterns include thoughts, expectations, emotions, and behavior in response to stressors and to tension. There seem to be some common patterns of coping with stress that lead more frequently to illness and difficulty than others. These are rooted in personality, but it is more useful to see coping style as a set of habits that can be modified and changed. Our stress level is in large part under our control.

In looking at the whole stress cycle, there are several clear avenues by which a person can reduce his or her stress level, or manage the stress more effectively:

- Reduce the pressure or demands from the environment
- Modify negative, self-critical, self-defeating, or other mental patterns that tend to create or amplify threats or dangers
- Cope actively and effectively with demands and situations that trigger the stress response, thereby turning it off and avoiding the buildup of tension
- Create supportive intimate and work relationships
- Practice effective techniques of tension management to avoid the negative effects of buildup of disabling tension

Each chapter of this book explains one of these areas, teaching ways to explore it and make changes.

STRESS AND HEALTH

As our lives change and society evolves, the diseases we succumb to change as well. While disease itself seems to be an unavoidable part of human life, the types of disease we face are a reflection of the problems of our society. In developing cultures the diseases are primarily of birth and early childhood, which are fatal to all but the heartiest infants, and infectious diseases that sweep through towns and cities.

In industrial society the awareness of nutrition and sanitation as health factors and the rise of technological medicine have enabled most children to survive, and have given us tools to control or manage some of the most severe infections and inherited diseases. More people live longer.

But this has caused a new set of problems. Organs in our body wear down unevenly, and those of us born with inherited weaknesses will begin to feel strain, pain, and breakdown in one or another part of the body as we age. The diseases we face today, known as the diseases of civilization because they are associated with industrialized society, are mainly due to degeneration and wearing down of parts of our body. While these illnesses can be managed by drugs and medical interventions, and to a degree negative effects like pain can be alleviated, these illnesses are not curable or reversible. While we can survive a heart attack, say, or live with diabetes, medical care does not "cure" us.

Everything we do, and everything we feel and experience, influences our health. For example, researchers have found that people are more likely to become ill under any of the following conditions:

- experiencing many changes—good or bad—in your life
- losing a spouse or someone you love
- not feeling connected to other people
- holding in feelings of anger and resentment
- pushing yourself without taking time to rest
- feeling helpless and not in control

These things happen to all of us at one time or another. So what can a person do to remain well?

First, it helps to be aware of the connection. When something happens to you, or you are doing something that you know puts you under stress and may lead to illness, then you need to take better care of yourself then and there. There is some evidence that illness and physical symptoms come about when we do not heed our body's subtle and gentle warnings. Thus if our lives are changing, or we feel that we are under a lot of stress and pressure, or we are experiencing emotional distress, then we need to think about making some changes in our lives.

The key to managing or holding off the breakdown of our bodies is not simply traditional medicine or health insurance; it lies in preventing damage from occurring for as long as possible. Those with a weak heart or stomach or muscle group need to practice preventive health care, because once the weakest link in the body goes, the rest of the body follows. In addition, as we live longer, preventive medicine may make the difference between a disabled and painful life or a vital and productive life. Over time the quality of life becomes an important factor, mere survival is not enough.

The breakdown of our body is the specific outcome of long-term wear and tear, in other words, stress. General stress of whatever type builds up if not managed effectively, leading to specific illnesses. Our illnesses result from our heredity and also from the way we take care of our body. A major contributor to illness is the presence of too much stress in our lives. Therefore, one of the major reasons for learning effective stress management is long-term preventive health care. In addition to helping our lives work better and feel better, stress management is the best thing we can do to optimize our health.

There is an emerging consensus among health leaders that preventive medicine emphasizing self-care is the major medical resource of the future.

SELF-MANAGEMENT AND SELF-RENEWAL

The president of a manufacturing firm manages many resources, organizes scores of people in complex tasks, and exerts control over a vast system that brings in materials, transforms them into products, and then extends out into the community through sales and marketing. It is odd that his mastery and control are only skin deep. When he develops chronic migraine headaches, or elevated blood pressure, or periodic stomach trouble, he feels helpless, frustrated, and unable to control them. While his mastery and control extend throughout his corporate empire and into the community, inside himself remains a mystery. Instead he seeks help from a physician who prescribes several types of medication to loosen the constriction in his head, to ease the pressure in his circulatory system, and to diminish his stomach's secretion of hormones.

A medical solution to his physical problems has certain consequences. First, the medications have long-term effects on his body that create further difficulties, and with continued use some medicines lose their effectiveness. But more important, the reasons behind his symptoms remain a mystery. Why does his head hurt and his stomach tighten when there are problems at the plant? If he seeks only a medical solution he will leave untouched the underlying conditions in his life that may be creating the symptoms.

This businessman wants to know whether his symptoms are "caused" by stress. He has learned to divide the world of health into two camps: "real" physical illnesses, and psychosomatic illnesses that are due to various kinds of emotional stress. Actually, there is no such dividing line. All difficulties, no matter what the ailment, are affected and often triggered by stress. For example, heart disease is due to many factors, all of which put strain on the circulatory system. These are hereditary, dietary, and sometimes also include lack of proper exercise, as well as the presence of chronic stress. Say a business disaster triggers a heart attack. Was stress the "cause" of it? Yes and no; it was one of several causes. A change in any one of the factors might have made his body that much more able to resist the stress of the disaster.

For this man's ailments medical treatment is only one part of health care. Why, we ask, can this man manage so much of his external world, coordinate so many people and products, yet be unable to extend his mastery to his inner world and learn to control his health? In the past there were good reasons for not extending our mastery to our inner worlds. But the medical problems we all face today cannot be overcome without lifting this veil that separates us from awareness and management of our physical and our psychological body processes.

Anyone who can manage other people has all the abilities and qualifications for self-management. When he decides that his health and well-being are too important to be left solely in the hands of a physician, he will discover new possibilities. He can learn to look inward and listen to his body, to become more sensitive to its needs, so that he can prevent symptoms like stomach cramps or headaches from developing. He can learn that his body *can* withstand an intense and difficult life-style. And he can explore ways to manage internal physical processes, learning skills to lower his blood pressure, ease tired muscles, limit stomach secretions, and other changes that materially affect his health, now and in the future. Finally, he can regulate his activities not only to attain the most effective organization, which will improve his own health, but also to help his employees manage their own stress.

This workbook contains a series of exercises and activities that can help every person to take control over the negative effects of their life stress and to manage their own health more effectively.

BURNOUT

Stress and pressure are givens in our lives. We cannot escape them by moving to the country or turning back the clock. Yet some people seem to thrive on pressure, while others cannot meet the demands and succumb to illness. We can think of the long-term outcomes of life under stress at two extremes—at the positive end are the survivors, who respond to pressures by thriving and achieving peak or optimal performance, while at the other extreme are those who fall apart and succumb to varieties of what has come to be called burnout. While we may be tempted to say that the differences lie in personality, individual talent, and constitutional factors—and there is some truth to this—recent research exploring how people respond to pressure and looking at people who achieve peak performance and those who burn out, suggests that where you lie on the continuum between burnout and peak performance is under your control. Self-awareness, self-renewal, and self-management are skills that can be learned, cultivated, and practiced.

Let us begin with one end of the scale. Burnout is a buzzword today, and many people react with a sigh of recognition when it is mentioned. Burnout was first mentioned by psychoanalyst Herbert

Freudenberger, and by psychologists Christina Maslach and Ayala Pines, in reference to professionals in human service. These professionals had entered their careers with great idealism and high expectations of helping people and doing meaningful work. Yet they encountered demands from clients that they could not meet, were frustrated by the bureaucracy, and sensed that their skill and dedication were not appreciated. As a result they withdrew emotionally from colleagues and clients, became apathetic, thought of their work as only a means of making money, and lost interest, energy, and dedication. They became burned out.

The same outcomes were seen in other professions. We have always known that clerical and assembly-line work are deadening, and the word "alienation" has been applied to the continued experience of such work. In addition other types of workers reported the experience of burnout. Generally, burnout seems to be the fatigue and frustration brought about by dedication to a job, a cause, a way of life, or even a relationship that is not bringing the expected reward. When one does not get what one wants or expects and feels trapped by obligation or economic circumstances in the situation, one responds with a withdrawal of energy characterized as burnout.

Herbert Freudenberger developed a burnout scale to assess the general level of burnout in all dimensions of life. See where you fit on the scale. While some researchers distinguish between job burnout and total life burnout, Freudenberger suggests that the phenomenon tends to generalize. Rarely is a person burned out at work yet energized and alive in his or her family or personal life. Job burnout affects personal life, although, as we will see in later chapters, supportive personal relationships can be a buffer against burnout.

If your score on the burnout scale is 30 or more, then you need to begin to ask yourself: **What in your life is wearing you down and what needs to be changed?** Even though this book concentrates primarily on burnout and stress in work settings, in fact the authors' view is that it is impossible to separate work from home life. The skills that overcome burnout in one setting are the same ones that work in the other.

Think back over your career, your time on the job, and try to see if there were clear stages of satisfaction. Was there an initial period of excitement and idealism, of energetic feeling? How did you respond to the frustrations, drawbacks, or conflicts in your job? What opportunities have you had to change these factors, and which of these have you not taken advantage of? As you will see, burnout is not something that lies outside yourself, in the nature of your job or life: it is an effect of inadequate responses to these factors. Behind the experience of burnout is a sense of personal powerlessness, a feeling that you cannot make a difference and change things, which tends to become a self-fulfilling prophecy. If you feel you are helpless, you become burned out, without ever discovering that you may be wrong. As the authors will show, your response to pressures makes the difference between burnout or peak performance.

EXERCISE 1

THE BURNOUT SCALE*

Review all of the parts of your life: work, social, and family. How have they changed over the last six to twelve months? Give yourself 0–5 points on each item. On items where things have remained as good as ever or even improved, give yourself 0 points. On items where things have deteriorated badly, take 5 points. In between would be 1–4 points.

1. Do you tire more easily? Feel fatigued rather than energetic? _____
2. Are people annoying you by telling you, "You don't look so good lately"? _____
3. Are you working harder and harder and accomplishing less and less? _____
4. Are you increasingly cynical and disenchanted? _____
5. Are you often invaded by a sadness you can't explain? _____
6. Are you forgetting (appointments, deadlines, personal possessions)? _____
7. Are you increasingly irritable? More short tempered? More disappointed in the people around you? _____
8. Are you seeing close friends and family members less frequently? _____
9. Are you too busy to do even routine things like make phone calls or read reports or send out your Christmas cards? _____
10. Are you suffering from physical complaints (aches, pains, headaches, a lingering cold)? _____
11. Do you feel disoriented when the activity of the day comes to a halt? _____
12. Is joy elusive? _____
13. Are you unable to laugh at a joke about yourself? _____
14. Does sex seem like more trouble than it's worth? _____
15. Do you have very little to say to people? _____

0–25	You're doing fine
26–35	There are things you should be watching
36–50	You're a candidate
51–65	You're burning out
65+	Take special note, distinct threats to your health and well-being

* H. J. Freudenberger and G. Richelson. *Burnout: The High Cost of High Achievement* (New York: Bantam Books, 1980).

15

PEAK PERFORMANCE

Stress is associated not only with distress, but also with excitement, achievement, and effective organization. In a study of major corporate leaders' attitudes toward stress, Herbert Benson found that many of them felt that creating stress and pressure in their organization was an important factor in creating effectiveness. They themselves felt that they thrived on the challenge of stress, and they instilled that pressure and challenge in their employees.

Like many commonsense insights the association of stress with optimal performance is partly correct and partly incorrect. It is true, for example, that positive stress ("eustress") is something that many people seek—excitement, risk, thrills, challenge, competition, and overcoming adversity. All of these positive stresses give our life flavor and meaning, and spur us on to important, creative, and satisfactory achievement. Stress seeking is a quality that helps to account for human beings' remarkable adaptiveness and accomplishments.

Yet there seems to be a line for each person where challenge becomes burden and excitement becomes fear. Hans Selye, for example, talks about individual differences in relation to stress. Some people, he notes, are turtles: they need a steady, predictable environment in which to shine. Others, including most corporate chiefs, are racehorses: they need a high level of stimulation, challenge, and change to bring out their best. The mistake is thinking that one climate serves all.

As we can see from the Performance Curve (Figure 1-3), there is an optimal level of stress for each person, at which he or she reaches peak performance. Effectiveness drops off with either too much or too little stress or pressure. Things can become too dull, just as they can become too stimulating. The task for each person, and for an organization as a whole, is to discover this optimal level.

A simple exercise can help. Remember some times when you were working at your best, when you were involved, challenged, and excited. Summon as much detail as possible. Now write down some of the qualities that stimulate you to maximum performance. What are the qualities of your environment? What sorts of pressures or deadlines spur you to action? What tasks energize you and which ones bore you? Do you work best alone or with others? What sort of help or guidance do you need?

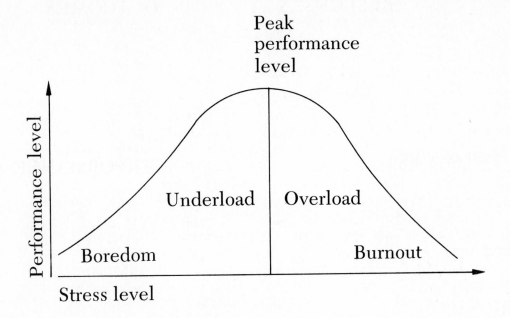

Figure 1-3: PERFORMANCE CURVE

Peak performance takes place for each person at a certain level of stress or pressure. If there is too little stress, things are boring and there is an underload. If there is too much stress or pressure, burnout or overload diminishes performance. The determination of each person's optimal stress level, and the creation of an environment that supports it, is an important aspect of effective stress management.

RESPONDING TO STRESS: OUR MODEL

In order to make our direction clearer, we present our model in blueprint form. Figure 1-4 looks at the various responses a person can make to the daily pressures of life.

The figure illustrates two broad styles of responding to ongoing pressures. There is the *defensive path* whereby a person remains unaware and unreflective concerning the effects of stress and his or her ways of responding to it. This path is characterized by denial and avoidance of the effects of one's behavior and the effects of stress on oneself. This person's characteristic responses to stress are reactive, consisting mainly of reflexes, methods of coping that were primarily learned early in life. Over time these ineffective responses lead to illness, distress, psychological and physical breakdown, and burnout.

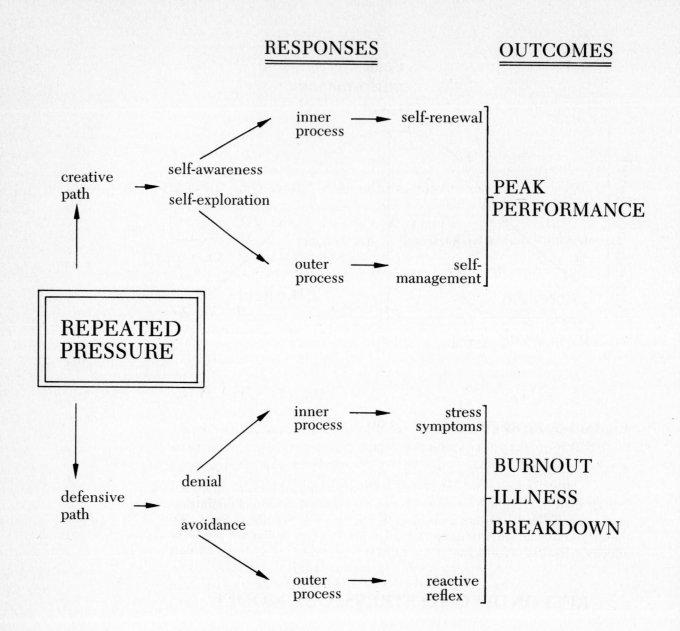

**Figure 1-4: CREATIVE AND DEFENSIVE RESPONSES
TO STRESS AND THEIR OUTCOMES**

The alternative response to stress is the *creative path,* in which a person utilizes self-awareness, the techniques of self-renewal, and the skills of self-management. This person moves in the direction of peak performance, and remains in balance in his or her life. By responding creatively the person combines self-care with the proper skills to complete tasks.

Comparative studies of burned-out professionals and managers and of those who exemplify outstanding performance and ability to resist stress have taught the authors much about how to help people move from one pathway to another. The authors have done research and worked individually with hundreds of executives, physicians, lawyers, clerical workers, and managers who are experiencing signs of burnout, and we have taught these people more creative responses to stress. In addition we have both spent considerable time in a newer line of research, looking at the qualities of exceptional people who are able to be at their most creative and still remain healthy and adapt to change. From the experiences of both types of people, the authors have distilled certain basic skills and principles that govern the transformation from a victim of burnout to a creator and achiever.

USING THIS BOOK: THE PROCESS OF CHANGE

The authors don't ask you merely to read this book. It is a workbook that requires your interaction. Each chapter contains self-assessment questions that ask you to explore some facet of your life. Each assessment helps you gather information about whether some dimensions of your life and your way of managing pressure cause you difficulty and contribute to burnout. If this is the case, the rest of that chapter helps you understand what the problems are about, and offers concrete steps you can take to overcome them. The attitude that you need to bring to this book is a willingness to experiment, to take risks, and to try new things. The authors are suggesting that you begin a process of change that may have profound effects on your life and work.

Before beginning, here are some guidelines for using this book. First, do not read it in one long sitting. You might begin by skimming the whole book and thinking about which sections seem most critical or important to you. Some people might need to learn self-renewal skills, others need self-management skills. The chapters can be done in any order. One way to know if a chapter is particularly relevant to you is to try the self-assessment exercises that are usually in the first section of a chapter. If you come out with a high score, you need work in that area. If your score is relatively low, skip to the next chapter.

Do the exercises and work through the material in each chapter in short study periods of perhaps a half hour to an hour. Set aside a little time each day to work on personal change. If you take special time and ask not to be interrupted, you will be showing yourself that you take this work, and yourself, seriously. You will be making a commitment to change. No changes, of course, occur overnight. They demand work, practice, self-reflection, and dedication.

This book was developed from workshops the authors have conducted for scores of companies and hundreds of individuals. All the material has been tested and refined for using on your own. The authors deeply believe in each person's ability to use such a program to create meaningful personal change.

As a further aid for training, cassette tapes of the exercises and lectures on each topic in the book, a *Personal Stress Explanation* which contains all the assessment exercises in a self-scoring booklet, and a *Trainer's Manual* for using the book as part of an organizational peak performance program can all be obtained from Essi Systems at 764 Ashbury Street, San Francisco, CA 94117, and from Learning for Health, 1314 Westwood Boulevard, Los Angeles, CA 90024.

The remainder of this book is organized into three parts. Part I, "Managing Change and Creating Personal Power," explores the ways that you can create more effective responses to your daily demands, changes, and pressures. The chapters in this section look at the types of pressure, demand, and change in your life, and at the internal and external strategies you can use to manage yourself most effectively. The skills for attaining personal power and active, helpful coping strategies are outlined.

Part II, "Sharing and Connecting," is about getting help and support from the people around you—at home, at work, and in the community. It is about connecting to others and creating positive, helpful, self-supporting relationships. In Part III, "Renewing Yourself," the focus shifts back to you. The techniques are self-renewal, in which you become aware of your inner self and its complex structure, and find ways to take better care of yourself. Self-care and self-renewal are more than physical hygiene. This process involves aligning your outer world to reflect your unique and special qualities. Finally, the conclusion is a chapter on peak performance, which presents ways that you can not only go beyond burnout, but also attain the most effective use of your abilities and creative potential.

Guidelines for Changing

Certain general principles apply to all efforts at personal change. These guidelines represent the experience of people who have changed many aspects of their lives. These guidelines should be applied to everything that follows:

1. *Make changes in small steps.* If you try to change everything at once, you feel helpless and overwhelmed. Think

about what you want to change, and then select a small but significant first step.

2. *Change one thing at a time.* Changing demands careful attention to one's goals. Few of us have the time or the energy to change several things at once. Also, the good feelings and success we achieve in one area are fuel for the next hurdle. Thinking of your entire change program as a ladder, which starts with the easiest steps and then builds to more (for you) difficult changes and tasks, is useful. Begin with the types of change you are most likely to be able to make, or which you expect to be the most pleasurable for you, and use what you learn about yourself to help you later scale the more difficult heights.

3. *Have clear, concrete, specific goals.* Telling yourself you want to, for example, deal better with stress is vague and confusing. What does it mean? Give yourself a clear concrete vision of what you want to achieve. List the specifics of what you want to change.

4. *Be aware of how you are when you begin.* Our general ideas of how we react to stress, for example, may be quite different from the reality. Before we begin to change, we need to be aware of current patterns. We do this by keeping a record of the type of behavior we wish to change. We may not be as bad as we think, or we may have an even greater problem than we believe. Either way, it is important to know.

5. *Offer rewards.* We love to get presents, and if we offer ourself rewards each time we meet a goal, we will be more likely to feel good about ourselves and persevere. Being nice to ourselves is what self-renewal is all about.

6. *Find a support person.* It's far easier to change if you have someone on the sidelines cheering for you, or if you have someone doing the same things alongside you. It is hard for a single member of a family to change any habit if the others are not encouraging and supportive. The most effective change program is one where you have a buddy whose job is to encourage you, check up on you, and share activities with you. If your buddy is trying to make similar changes in his or her life, the partnership is even better.

7. *Expect failures and relapses.* We all experience failure. But failure is a matter of degree. If you don't exercise for a few weeks, or neglect your projected tasks on a weekend, that is not failure. Change is always a matter of ups and downs, not a smooth course. You can help yourself

by expecting to encounter difficulty and have relapses. You can help yourself by planning days off on, say, weekends, or by simply picking yourself up if you have veered from your plan and getting back on course. Soon a slight relapse will not divert you from your overall goal, and you will find that flexibility does not cause you to lose sight of, or your ability to achieve, your goals.

8. *Use positive imagery and self-talk.* You can encourage or discourage yourself by the way you talk and think. We are always talking to ourselves, and in a positive peak performance program we need to give ourselves a constant diet of positive suggestions and encouragement, and continually imagine how we will feel, look, and act when we are healthy. This includes the use of positive mental imagery as a way of programming our mental attitudes, which in turn are linked to habitual behavior. Don't demean, punish, or put yourself down for not doing something.

Part I

MANAGING CHANGE
AND CREATING
PERSONAL POWER

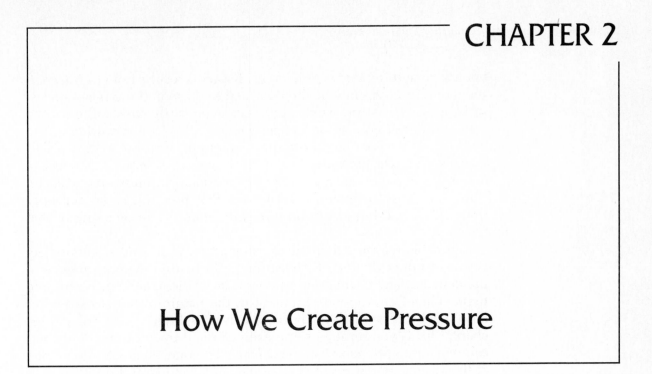

CHAPTER 2

How We Create Pressure

STRESSORS: THE PULL OF THE ENVIRONMENT

Take a few moments to remember some of the recent situations you found demanding or difficult. What made them stressful? Everything that seems stressful to us involves a change or event that demands a corresponding response. For example, when a co-worker is absent, the event is stressful if we are forced to adjust our workload accordingly. Or when somebody seems to challenge our competence or ability, the stress-provoking demand is for us to prove ourselves.

Our lives are composed of thousands of demands, pressures, and changes that force us to adapt and change many times a day. The pace of change in our lives and the multiple sources of pressure upon us make modern life uniquely stressful.

Added to that is the continual assault on our senses. Noise, traffic, poor air, and a crush of people can overload our nervous system, and the more stresses, the less we are able to cope with one more thing.

We pay a price for living in a free, loosely regulated society. The pressure of making the right choice among so many offered and the uncertainty of jobs and relationships mean that many of us cannot let down our guards and feel safe. Disaster can strike at any time. Conflict, too, is always part of our lives. At home and at work the pressure of angry demands, needs, and expectations of other people wear us out. It often seems as if getting things for ourselves can come only at the expense of somebody else, or through conflict with another.

But when we look more closely at the pressures and demands on us—our *stressors*—we see that the picture is incomplete. Pressure is not just something that is done to us. Rather it results from us *interacting with* our environment. Being asked to do something is not necessarily a demand or pressure, nor is this necessarily stressful to us. We can ignore the request, or we can welcome it as a recognition of our worth. If we experience the request in either of these ways, we will feel only a slight pressure. But suppose we see a request as a test of our ability and feel that a job, a course grade, or a friendship is at stake. Then the pressure mounts. So we see that pressure stems not only from a demand, but also from our perception of the meaning of that demand.

For this reason it is hard to categorize events and situations according to their degree of stressfulness. Pressure is a consequence of the demands and changes, our perception of them, and our reaction to them. Therefore, the measurement of the nature of our stress and of how much pressure there is in our lives is highly subjective. This chapter leads you through some exercises and inventories so that you can diagnose your *personal stress level*. The questions ask you to look at the various pressures, changes, demands, and stressful events that occur in your life, and to explore which of them create the most pressure.

This chapter is organized into several parts. First you will look at some of the major sources of pressure in your work and personal life. Next you will explore some of your major stressors, especially those at work, and your characteristic responses. You will begin to draw your personal stress response profile. Then you look at the recent changes in your life that create pressure for you to adjust to them. Finally you examine the subjective side of stressful events—the way your own internal conversation with yourself (your expectations, beliefs, thoughts, and ways of seeing things) can create or minimize pressure and stress.

This chapter probes the boundary between you and your world. If burnout is the outcome of poor management of your life, then the way that you allow yourself to become pressured, distressed, and upset is an important starting point for a program to overcome it. Stressors lie neither wholly in the world nor wholly in yourself. Rather stressors, which trigger stress, lie in the interaction between you and the world.

Sources of Stress

Many of us see pressures and demands as one big sticky mass, without shape or form, and each added incident just seems to stick along with the whole. While things may *feel* that way, this view leaves us even more overwhelmed and helpless. What can we do, we ask ourselves, since the mass is just too large to budge?

In fact, our stressors—pressures, demands, and changes—have a structure and pattern. When we look at them closely, we can find specific types of pressure that predominate, and we can take steps to manage each appropriately and effectively. The first step is to recognize your own particular types of pressure.

We can place the stressors in our lives into two broad categories. First there are the *chronic, ongoing pressures*. These include the daily hassles, the irritating, frustrating, depressing, and upsetting incidents that occur regularly in our lives. They take place at work, at home, in the community, and in our relationships. They include small things like traffic jams, which, while predictable, are nonetheless stressful, and ongoing pressures like excessive demands for work performance.

The second category of stressors is *episodic*. These are the crises, changes, unplanned incidents, and planned transitions that take us from one life situation to another and demand adjustment and coping.

The distinction between ongoing and episodic stressors is important for several reasons. First of all it is important to know whether the pressures you face are due to particular crises that are time limited, and thus can be overcome, or are regular parts of your life. The process of coping with chronic, ongoing stressors is different from coping with discrete crises. An ongoing stressor cannot usually be overcome; rather it must be met and managed in a self-supportive way. If you cannot stop the demands of a job or of your daily commute, you need to find ways to manage your responses to the demands and the traffic to preserve your well-being. So the first exercises in this chapter explore the source and nature of your major stressors.

We are always under the spell of many chronic, ongoing stressors and, much of the time, some episodic incidents and changes as well. Sometimes it is not the particular changes, but the cumulative effect of one on top of another that does us in and leaves us feeling burned out and drained.

In addition to the two categories of stressors, stress occurs in different settings. The two major settings are our work world and our personal family world. Exercise 2 contains four boxes. Think of the various sources and types of stressors that you are experiencing in your life right now and enter them in the appropriate box. Underline the stressors that are the most pressing, severe, or difficult for you to manage.

A clear picture will begin to emerge of the major sources of stress in your life, and whether they are chronic or result from episodic changes or crises that might be overcome and adjusted to.

Settings for Stress.   The two most common areas of stress in our lives are work and family. Most of us can single out one or the other of these areas as the major source of our problems. An unfortunate few feel that their stress arises in both settings.

There is really no way to compare the actual degree of stress different people experience. Everyone's stress feels big. The impor-

EXERCISE 2:   PERSONAL SOURCES OF STRESS

	WORK/CAREER	FAMILY/PERSONAL
EPISODIC	1. 2. 3. 4. 5. 6.	1. 2. 3. 4. 5. 6.
CHRONIC	1. 2. 3. 4. 5. 6.	1. 2. 3. 4. 5. 6.

tant question is not the quantity of your stress, but rather its effects on your body and your life.

Exercise 3 consists of two lists of pressures and sources of stress, at work and at home. For each statement estimate how much pressure it adds to your life. When you have completed the scale, you will have some sense of the patterns of your stress. These patterns are the places to focus your attention when you begin to think about making changes.

Job Stress. Our perceptions of stress on the job are usually hampered by outmoded, mechanistic conceptions of work and organizations. The misconception is that the organization is a firmly defined, almost solid structure, consisting of jobs that are specified by role slots, all connected into sections, work groups, and divisions. People are expected to fit into defined jobs and to conform their behavior to what is expected. The organization is inflexible and difficult if not impossible to change. We expect to feel resentful and alienated from such a self-limiting and constricting situation.

New visions of jobs and organizations have emerged that offer a more realistic perception of the person and the organization. In these newer views the organization is seen more as a web of fluid alliances, which shifts to accommodate new energy and people. People and organizations are organic wholes. The organization and the job role are not as firmly fixed or clearly defined, but rather represent a human network that is organized around central goals, cultural norms, and values and pathways toward these goals. In this vision the human being has more power, meaning, and influence over the organization.

We all experience job stress. We feel it in our bodies and in our feelings, energy level, and response to our work. We are familiar with these reactions. But we need to step back a bit to understand more clearly how the stress arises from our interaction with our work setting.

Exercise 4 is an inventory that looks at some of the common sources of job stress. For each job-related stressor indicate how often you feel that way or have that sense or experience.

Relating to Job Stress. We are not robots who are forced into job slots that pressure us, alienate us, and eventually burn us out when we are exchanged for another worker. On the contrary, the way to look at job stress is as a result of our personal interaction with our job and organization. Work is a situation where we are negotiating, making requests, and undertaking tasks for other people. By looking at the questions in the Job Stress Inventory, we begin to see that job stress results from many discrete, particular situations and procedures. Some of them are within our control and, once noticed, can be changed through negotiation and interaction. Others are less controllable.

The first step in dealing with life stress is to break it down into its
(text continues on page 35)

EXERCISE 3

SETTINGS FOR STRESS

The following scales indicate pressures and demands in the two central environments in your life. For each question, estimate the degree of pressure or demand a situation places upon you. Then total your scores for each section.

I. Work and Career	Severe	Moderate	A Little	None
1. Too many tasks or responsibilities	4	3	2	1
2. Confused or ambiguous roles or expectations	4	3	2	1
3. Conflicting or competing demands	4	3	2	1
4. Conflict with supervisor or superior	4	3	2	1
5. Conflict or difficulty with co-workers	4	3	2	1
6. Dull, boring, or repetitive work tasks	4	3	2	1
7. No rewards for work well done	4	3	2	1
8. Competition between co-workers	4	3	2	1
9. No opportunity for advancement	4	3	2	1
10. No room for creativity and personal input	4	3	2	1
11. No input to decisions affecting your work	4	3	2	1
12. Difficult commuting	4	3	2	1
13. Deadline pressure	4	3	2	1
14. Many organizational or job task changes	4	3	2	1
15. Difficult or distracting work environment	4	3	2	1
16. Loss of commitment or idealism	4	3	2	1
17. Confused or unclear expectations about tasks	4	3	2	1

I. Work and Career (continued)	Severe	Moderate	A Little	None
18. Inadequate salary for your needs or expectations	4	3	2	1 *KB*
19. Lack of friendships or communication with co-workers	4	*K* 3	2	*B* 1

40

TOTAL I

II. Household, Family and Community

	Severe	Moderate	A Little	None
1. Not enough money	*B* 4	3	2	*K* 1
2. Conflict with spouse	4	3	2	*KB* 1
3. Conflict over household tasks	4	3	*B* 2	*K* 1
4. Problems or conflict with children	4	3	*B* 2	*K* 1
5. Pressure from relatives or in-laws	4	3	2	*KB* 1
6. Household repairs	4	3	2	*KB* 1
7. Not enough leisure time	4	*B* 3	*K* 2	1
8. Sexual conflict or frustration	4	3	2	*KB* 1
9. Dangerous or stressful surroundings and neighborhood	4	*K* 3	2	*B* 1
10. Conflict or falling out with close friend or relative	4	3	*BK* 2	1
11. Personal problem causing strain in family	4	*B* 3	2	*K* 1
12. No babysitters; difficult to get away from home	4	3	2	*KB* 1

26

TOTAL II

A total of over 40 on Part I or over 30 on Part II indicates significant sources of stress in your work or household environment. You need to learn to manage them well.

E X E R C I S E   4

JOB STRESS INVENTORY

I. Work Environment	Almost Always	Frequently	Sometimes	Never
1. My working conditions are hard on my body	4	3	2	1
2. My work is dangerous or hazardous	4	3	2	1
3. I feel pressure	4	3	2	1
4. I am near toxic substances at work	4	3	2	1
5. My workplace is bleak, uncomfortable, or depressing	4	3	2	1
TOTAL I				

II. Organizational Environment	Almost Always	Frequently	Sometimes	Never
1. Office politics interfere with my work	4	3	2	1
2. I can't get the information I need for my work	4	3	2	1
3. What is expected or how to do things is not clear to me	4	3	2	1
4. There is a competitive, backbiting atmosphere	4	3	2	1
5. I don't have the resources I need to get my job done (e.g., time, money, help)	4	3	2	1
6. I do not participate in decisions that affect my work and job	4	3	2	1

II. Organizational Environment (continued)	Almost Always	Frequently	Sometimes	Never
7. Things are changing too fast at work (new products, technologies, management team)	4	3	2	1 *KB*
8. My work does not provide clear or reasonable pathways for advancement	4	3	2	1 *KB*
TOTAL II				

11

III. Job Role

	Almost Always	Frequently	Sometimes	Never
1. It is not clear what is expected of me	4	3	2	1
2. Too many things are expected of me	4	3 *B*	2	1
3. I find myself being asked to do conflicting things	4	3 *B*	2	1
4. I feel overloaded at work	4	3 *B*	2	1
5. My job expectations are changing	4	3	2 *B*	1
TOTAL III				

11

IV. Self and Role Fit

	Almost Always	Frequently	Sometimes	Never
1. I don't like what I do	4	3	2	1 *KB*
2. My job is boring and meaningless	4	3	2	1 *KB*
3. I have the wrong job for me	4	3	2	1 *KB*
4. My job doesn't utilize my skills and abilities	4	3	2	1 *KB*

4

IV. Self and Role Fit (continued)	Almost Always	Frequently	Sometimes	Never
5. I have ethical problems with what I do	4	3	2	1
6. What I wanted/expected from my job has not turned out to be there	4	3	2	1
7. I am not able to advance as much as I would like	4	3	2	1
8. I have been passed over for promotion	4	3	2	1
TOTAL IV				
V. Interpersonal Environment				
1. I have too much responsibility for others	4	3	2	1
2. Relationships between co-workers are poor or full of conflict	4	3	2	1
3. Other people at work create conflict for me	4	3	2	1
4. I am not clear where I stand, whether my work is respected by supervisors	4	3	2	1
5. Too many people tell me what to do	4	3	2	1
6. I am pressured by demands of clients/customers	4	3	2	1
7. I have too much or too little contact with other people	4	3	2	1
TOTAL V				
TOTAL I–V				

A total of more than 15 on sections I or III, or more than 20 on sections II, IV, or V, suggests that you are under considerable stress in that area. If you have considerable stress in several areas, you need to make some changes in your response to your work.

component parts and to see specifically where it comes from. Thus when we see, for example, that our job stress results from difficulties in personal relationships and an organizational environment that pits people against each other and discourages cooperation, we can then begin to devise ways to change this. The chapters that follow detail ways to create strategies to change specifics of situations that otherwise would create personal distress and lead to burnout.

Job stress results from a number of points of intersection between you and your organization. First there is your physical work environment. While you might regard this as relatively fixed, company after company has begun to pay attention to the effects of environment on productivity and well-being. The second aspect of the work environment is the structure, culture, and values of the organization itself. These include its ideas of what a good worker is, what it expects from people, how it sees its mission in the world. The organizational culture has recently become a focus of management concern, as studies have suggested that certain sets of values seem to characterize successful and innovative companies, while others are impediments. Generally, as we will see later, there is a clear connection between high-stress-producing environments and low effectiveness.

Your job is made up of expectations, tasks, and personal relationships that you are expected to manage and fulfill. Every job role is changed by the person who enters it. However, some people enter a job and regard the role as fixed, while others see every expectation and task as something that can be negotiated or questioned. Reality is probably somewhere in between. Another question about job role that directly pertains to work stress is how well your job fits you. Is the job one you enjoy, that you can do well, that challenges you? If the answer is no, then tasks that another person might not find stressful become boring, frustrating, or difficult.

A final dimension of job stress is the person-to-person environment. The nature of the personal relationships among people can be a source of distress or a source of strength. How much information people share, how helpful they are, and how clear evaluations and expectations are, all affect your job stress.

Thus the stress you feel is a composite score, felt by your body and your psyche, consisting of the effects of all the interactions and the environment of your workplace on you. It is not inevitable; neither, as we will see, is it something that must simply be accepted.

What Makes Pressure Stressful?   Look over your lists of stressors and sources of personal stress. You experience certain events that cause you stress. You might see, for example, that things bring you into conflict with other people, threatening your personal interests; you might see the press of having to do more than you can do or not knowing which task to do first as your most prevalent form of stress. General themes arise.

Stressors affect us because they force us to adjust or respond to them. Whether the demand is one we make on ourselves—such as an internal pressure to excel—or comes from the environment—such as competition with a co-worker for a promotion, or too many cars trying to get to the same place—our body must respond to it. In addition to whatever action we take to manage or overcome the stressor, our body also triggers a psychophysiological stress response to each of these situations. So we need to take care of the situation itself, as well as manage our body's typical overreaction. Therefore, stressors demand that we exercise effective external and internal management, what we call self-management of our response to the situation, and what we call self-renewal in response to the needs of our body for care.

Stressors represent challenges to our lives and livelihood. As human beings we face not only challenges to our physical well-being, but also challenges to our emotional well-being and self-esteem. Pressures and demands become stressful because we have to respond at the same time as maintaining our well-being and self-esteem against both real and possible (or even potential or imagined) threats.

While any external change or demand can be perceived as a source of stress, the majority of our life stresses fall into several categories:

1. *Loss:* The loss (or threat of loss) of someone or something we are attached to is painful, and we need to go through a period of mourning, sadness, or depression while making minor or major adjustments in our lives.

2. *Threat:* Whether the threat is to our self-esteem or to our person, the resulting stress response in our body is the same.

3. *Frustration:* Anyone or anything that, even potentially, seems to prevent us from meeting our basic needs or getting what we want is frustrating. We feel the most stress when something blocks our path and we feel that we are helpless to do anything about it.

4. *Uncertainty:* A situation that merely implies possible threat, loss, harm, or frustration can be especially stressful. Our imaginations help us to be creative; they also allow us to worry about and anticipate all manner of disasters. To our bodies the imagined danger and reality are the same: the stress response is triggered.

Hassles of Life. Most stressors are not momentous or a crisis; rather they consist of irritating, frustrating, distressing, unexpected, or difficult incidents—the hassles of daily life. Psychologist Richard Lazarus studied the effects of these everyday hassles and found that they had a direct influence on health and well-being.

His research also focused on incidents that are the opposite of hassles, which he labels "uplifts"—pleasant, happy, satisfying experiences. Uplifts can serve to balance the hassle side of life, and may perhaps also serve as insulators or buffers against the negative effects of hassles.

Lazarus studied hassles and uplifts in several groups of people. He found few commonalities in diaries that people kept of each day's hassles and uplifts. However, here are his lists of the most frequently named hassles and uplifts among middle-aged men and women who kept track for a year:

HASSLES	UPLIFTS
1. Concern about weight	1. Relating well with spouse or lover
2. Health of family	2. Relating well with friends
3. Rising prices	3. Completing a task
4. Home maintenance	4. Feeling healthy
5. Too many things to do	5. Getting enough sleep
6. Misplacing things	6. Eating out
7. Yard work	7. Meeting responsibilities
8. Property, investment, taxes	8. Visiting, phoning, or writing someone
9. Crime	9. Spending time with family
10. Physical appearance	10. Pleasing home environment

If you think about the pressure you are under, you will probably sense that the daily hassles weigh more heavily than the episodic life changes. Think back over the past month and make a list of regular hassles. Think about the things that frustrate, pressure, and irritate you at work and at home. These can include the things you think about as well as actual situations—*anything* that hassles you. Rank the hassles in order, from the most severe and disruptive to the least frustrating. Then look again at each of the hassles in your life, and write down some things that you could do to respond more effectively or take better care of these situations.

The other side of the coin is the uplifts, the pleasant, revitalizing, satisfying events, thoughts, and situations. Make a second list, this time of the uplifts you recall in the past month. Rank this list, too, with the most pleasant ones first. Now think of how you might arrange your life to have more uplifts, which might be an antidote to some of the frustrating and stressful hassles.

Hassles, worries, frustrations, and obstacles contribute significantly to our overall stress level. Some of them are of course beyond our control, but many take place within our mind and can be modified. Also, when we look at hassles, we see that many of them stem from the way we see things and where we focus our attention. As we will see later, these are aspects of our stress level that we can modify.

Exploring Your Reaction to Stressors

The most important thing to learn about the stressors in our lives —whether they are daily hassles or major life changes—is the way that we respond to them. Our responses are largely under our control and we can make them more effective or less effective. In this section we move from looking at the sources of stress in themselves, to looking at stressful situations from the vantage point of our responses to them.

We need to be aware of the stages of our responses. First is the often neglected period just prior to the stressful situation. Could the situation have been foreseen, and if we had foreseen it, might we have planned an effective response? How do we relate to situations when they come up—how does our body respond, what do we say to ourselves, what do we feel, and finally what do we do? Responses are not unchangeable. Starting in childhood, we have learned and developed certain habitual styles of response to various situations. These habits often become dysfunctional, especially by the time we are faced with adult realities and responsibilities. We need to change some basic habitual ways of dealing with stressful situations when we find that these habits tend to do us in, rather than support us.

In this section you will compile a Personal Stress Log to help you look at the regular situations that cause you stress and your response to them. From this log you can discover your response habits.

One of the authors' major goals is to help you move from a perception that stress is something that happens to you—you are its victim— to a knowledge that stress involves your own reaction to the world around you, and that reaction is alterable. To help you do this, you need to keep a daily log of stressful situations for at least one or two weeks.

Each time you face a stressful incident, take a moment to look at yourself and examine your responses. What was the trigger? What did you think and feel? How did you respond? How did others around you respond to your response? How effective was your interaction? What were the incident's negative effects on you? Asking these questions will make you sensitive to yourself in a new way, helping you to see how many different stages and possibilities are contained in a single situation.

Begin your Personal Stress Log by noting and exploring each event. Patterns in your perceptions and responses will begin to emerge. These are helpful in planning ways to change your response. After you have kept your log for a while, you can take some of the situations and answer some important questions about them, which will help to advance your analysis of your stress.

E X E R C I S E 5

PERSONAL STRESS LOG

Carry the log with you during the day. After any incident that leaves you feeling upset, distressed, angry, pressured, aroused, anxious, or frustrated, fill out one row of the log. After a few days you will have an ongoing record of stressful incidents in your life and your responses to them.

In each column indicate the following for each incident:

1. The date, day of the week, and time.
2. A few words about the nature of the event, so that you can remember it when you go over the log later on.
3. Your estimate of how distressing the incident was, on a scale of 1 to 10, with 1 indicating a mild distress and 10 a severe upset.
4. A few words about what you did, your own response and activity in the situation—before, during, and directly after it.
5. Your thoughts and feelings, the things that you said to yourself and felt during and after the incident.
6. How the incident left you feeling, physically and emotionally; its cost to you.

After keeping the log for a while, fill out the next scale, Qualities of Stressful Situations, for each incident. This is a further exploration and evaluation of such incidents.

PERSONAL STRESS LOG

Day/Time	Event	Distress Level (1–10)	What You Did	What You Thought/Felt	Your Physical Response

Use these questions and answers to explore other stressful situations and stressors in your life right now. Evaluate each stressor along these dimensions.

Your stress level is not necessarily increased the higher you get on the scale. Many factors affect the stress level in addition to the situation itself. However, let us review what is important about each of these dimensions.

The degree of pressure is your estimate of how much a stressful situation affects you. The higher your score, the more important it is that you do something about a situation. For many minor pressures putting them aside may be the best strategy. Major pressures usually cannot be avoided and must be resolved directly.

We can divide stressful situations into those which are episodic and those which are ongoing. Ongoing pressures may need general strategies for us to cope with them, lest they wear us down.

When we think about it, many unexpected pressures and situations can be anticipated. Like any situation, good or bad, the more we anticipate and plan for it, the more easily we can cope with it or enjoy it. Unexpected situations demand more from us because our body and our expectations are not prepared.

Some stressors are unavoidable, like noise levels on the street, while others can be avoided or changed. Many of us spend too much time trying to change things that cannot be changed, instead of doing something about those situations that can be modified.

When something can be done in a situation, then we need to take direct action. When we are in a situation that we cannot change or influence, then all we can do is take care of our bodies and try to bring ourselves back to baseline levels of rest. Failure to take action is a primary factor in creating stress-management problems. On reflection, in many of the situations that we initially define as being difficult or impossible to manage we may actually have considerable influence. We need to look closely at our perceptions of personal power and ability to control, manage, and influence the events around us.

Your Stress Response Profile. Now that you have explored your responses to stressful events in several ways, reread your logs and records. Summarize your style of responding to stress in Exercise 7 according to these guidelines:

> *Frequency:* How many times in a day do you encounter distress?

> *Severity:* How severe is the buildup of stress? How distressing are the worst incidents?

> *Anticipation:* Do you expect the incidents to develop, or are they unexpected? Are they isolated or ongoing? If they

(text continues on page 44)

EXERCISE 6

QUALITIES OF STRESSFUL SITUATIONS

Despite their almost infinite variety, the stressful situations we encounter have certain important qualities that bear on our attempt to find ways to decrease their effects on our bodies.

Make a list of some recent stressful situations. Now take the most difficult or pressing source of stress and answer these questions:

1. How much pressure did the situation place on me, compared with other stressful situations I have faced?

1	25		75	100
low		medium		high

2. Is the situation a single episode, not likely to be repeated, or a general, ongoing source of pressure?

1	25		75	100
episode				ongoing

3. To what degree could I have anticipated the event, or to what degree was it unanticipated or unexpected?

1	25		75	100
anticipated, predictable				unexpected, unforeseen

4. To what degree do I feel that I could have changed, resolved, or influenced the situation?

1	25		75	100
easy to change		hard to change		impossible to change

5. To what degree did I respond or act directly on the situation in an attempt to resolve it, or to what degree did I avoid, deny, or do nothing about it?

1	25		75	100
direct action				avoid, deny

QUALITIES OF STRESSFUL SITUATIONS

Description of Incident	Degree of Pressure	Episode/ Chronic	Anticipated/ Unexpected	Degree of Control	Direct Action/ Avoidance
1.					
2.					
3.					
4.					
5.					
6.					
7.					
8.					
9.					
AVERAGES	—	—	—	—	—

Scoring: Each column is scored from 0 to 100. The low end of the scale indicates that the situation was experienced as low pressure, an isolated episode, anticipated, easy to change or control, or one in which you took direct action. The high end of the scale indicates the opposite pole: high pressure or stress, a chronic and often repeated situation, unexpected, difficult or impossible to control or change, and you avoided doing anything about it. The lower scores are generally associated with less difficulty or damage to health. If your high scores are in one or two particular areas, focus on that quality in your work to modify your stress response.

are unexpected, can you learn how to see potential stressful events before they happen?

Sense of control: How many of the events that distress you can be controlled or changed by you, and how many cannot? Look at the most stressful situations and think about how you might create more control over them. How might you plan to cope with those events which you cannot influence?

Engaging or avoiding: Is your tendency to respond to situations by actively doing something about them, or to avoid the situation altogether?

Types of problem situations: What kinds of situations cause you distress? Where do you tend to encounter them?

Problem responses: What are the things you do in stressful situations that create difficulty for you?

Desired changes: What is the thing that you would most like to change about your response to stressful situations?

Thinking about these questions, or writing down your reflections, is a good way to become familiar with your usual coping responses and begin to brainstorm about ways to modify them.

Exploring Your Performance Under Pressure. When our stress levels become too high over prolonged time, we experience what Hans Selye labeled the exhaustion stage of the stress response. Exhaustion demands time off for recovery, and some of us never fully recover our previous energy levels. It makes sense, therefore, to build in rest breaks when we know we are going through a heavy workload.

We also should monitor our body's physiological response during a stress-inducing situation. In this way we can try to regulate our stress level before it becomes a problem. One way to increase self-awareness is to pose a series of questions. First, ask yourself: **How stressful is this situation going to be?**

If you can anticipate that a situation is potentially very stressful, this is the time to become alert and aware of what is happening to your body and take appropriate steps. Next ask yourself: **How much stress am I experiencing right now?**

Because our respiratory patterns are the most accessible of all stress indicators to control, it is easiest to pay special attention to breathing. In particular, ask yourself: **What's happening to my breathing right now? How is my behavior being affected right now?**

In a stressful situation you are likely to notice one of these things about your breathing: it seems to have stopped; it has become very shallow; or it has become more rapid. Whatever your combination of sensations, you will be impressed with how dramatically different your respiration is, compared with those situations when you are relaxed.

In a high-stress situation the next questions to ask are: **What can I do right now to respond to the situation? Can I do anything to change it?** and/or **What can I do to change my body's response?**

Sometimes it isn't possible to change or to leave a stressful situation. In this case then, ask: **What can I do to accept the situation? How can I change my attitude about it? Can I somehow redefine the situation so that it takes on a different meaning for me?**

Unfortunately, most situations are not easily changed or even within our sphere of influence. Therefore, changing the response to the situation is frequently the only approach we can take. **Since I can't change the situation, what value is there in getting excited or tense? Realistically, what is the proper level of stress for this situation?** If you have exceeded the "proper level," you are wasting valuable energy, and you are setting yourself up to become fatigued, emotionally upset, or physically depleted or ill. Posed another way, the questions are: **Is this the best way to treat myself right now?** and **What are the costs I am going to pay for allowing myself to get so stressed?**

After you have decided that action is required, begin to focus on your breathing patterns. At first don't make any effort to change them, just notice them. This simple shift of awareness will have an almost immediate effect. Now begin consciously to regulate your breathing. Allow your abdomen to relax. Imagine how your diaphragm is pushing down on your viscera, and as your abdominal muscles relax, your abdomen slightly extends. Begin to breathe slowly in a consciously regulated pattern. There's no need to stop focusing on the situation you are confronting; merely add another layer of awareness to your participation in this situation by watching your body. The following chapter presents ways to modify your response to stress, and Chapter 7, ways to modify your body's responses.

The Costs of Change

The type of stressor that has been most widely studied is life crises and changes. Researchers Thomas Holmes and Richard Rahe were struck by how the presence of many life changes is often followed by serious as well as minor illnesses. People who experience several changes—negative *or* positive—in the course of the year have a greater risk of becoming ill. This relationship obtains in all kinds of illnesses. For example, college football players who had the most changes in the year preceding the football season had a disproportionate share of injuries.

Exercise 7 helps you to estimate the effect of recent changes in your life. Has your past year been stable and consistent or has it had many major or minor changes? If you have had many changes, you are not alone.

What should you do if your life is full of changes? Change does not automatically result in illness. Rather many changes lower your resistance and you therefore have to take special care of your body. Anticipating future illness and trying to protect yourself is one of the cornerstones of self-care.

Change and Adjustment.   Many people who have several life changes or a high score on the adjustment scale begin to fear for their health. They come to the erroneous conclusion that change in itself is harmful to their health, like tobacco. Indeed changes and daily demands create pressure both on our bodies and our psyches as we struggle to adjust. However, research on coping with stress affirms that it is not so much how many pressures and changes we experience, but how we look at them, relate to them, and manage their effects.

The purpose of measuring the degree of outside pressure—stressors—in our lives is to begin the process of sensitizing us to the effects of demands upon us. The goal is awareness, not creating anxiety or plans for escape. For many of us change and pressure are also sources of challenge, novelty, excitement, and creative involvement. A life without change and demands would not allow us to utilize our creativity, our natural life energy, and such a life would be boring and unstimulating. However, increasing our awareness of stressors allows us to think about the effectiveness of our coping. For example, now that we know that change creates pressure, we can anticipate future changes and take special care of our bodies and special steps to manage the situation. Or we can begin to think of ways to deal with chronic daily frustration, hassles, and demands.

The Experience of Loss.   One type of change is particularly stressful and difficult: the experience of loss. Of course, the loss of someone you love is a devastating and painful experience. But there are other kinds of losses as well. There is the loss of a job, or even the loss of possibility of a promotion you were expecting. There is the loss of a friend or colleague who moves away. There is the loss of something that you were especially attached to, perhaps through theft.

Any loss leaves a vacuum in your life. A space and time that was filled pleasantly is now empty. It is reasonable to feel some pain and sad feelings, which may last a year or more for the loss of a loved one. After a loss we need to go through a process of grieving, in which we let go of the person (or thing) that was lost. It is a process of remembering and saying good-bye. Curiously, there is a clear grieving process associated with loss of work or opportunity, which is often complicated by anger and personal shame or feelings of inadequacy and self-blame. Be aware that such feelings are natural and necessary in overcoming a loss.

(text continues on page 49)

EXERCISE 7

ADJUSTMENT TO RECENT LIFE CHANGES

This scale estimates the amount of change in your recent life, and the energy it has taken for you to adjust to it.

In the list below check the "Event Occurred" column if the event in question has happened to you within the past *eighteen months*. (The column marked "Your Adjustment Score" will be explained after you have gone through the whole checklist.)

	Event Occurred	Your Adj. Score
Health		
1. An illness or injury that kept you in bed a week or more, or took you to the hospital	_____	_____
2. A major change in eating habits	_____	_____
3. A major change in sleeping habits	_____	_____
4. A change in your usual type and/or amount of recreation	_____	_____
Work		
5. Changed to a new type of work	_____	_____
6. Changed your work hours or conditions	_____	_____
7. Increase or decrease on work responsibilities (promotion, demotion, transfer)	_____	_____
8. Troubles with co-workers	_____	_____
9. A major business readjustment	_____	_____
10. Retired	_____	_____
11. Experienced being fired or laid off from work	_____	_____
12. Taken courses or studied to help you in your work	_____	_____
Home and Family		
13. A change in residence	_____	_____
14. A change in family "get-togethers"	_____	_____
15. A major change in the health or behavior of a family member (illness, accident, drug or disciplinary problems, etc.)	_____	_____

	Event Occurred	Your Adj. Score

Home and Family *(cont.)*

16. Home improvements or other household change   ———   ———
17. Death of a spouse   ———   ———
18. Death of close family member (relationship: ———)   ———   ———
19. Death of a close friend   ———   ———
20. Change in your parents' marital status (divorce, remarriage)   ———   ———
21. Marriage   ———   ———
22. Arguments with your spouse   ———   ———
23. In-law problems   ———   ———
24. Separation or reconciliation with your spouse   ———   ———
25. A gain of a new family member (birth, adoption, a relative moving in with you)   ———   ———
26. Spouse beginning or ceasing work outside the home   ———   ———
27. Pregnancy in family   ———   ———
28. Child leaving home   ———   ———
29. Miscarriage or abortion   ———   ———
30. Birth of a grandchild   ———   ———
31. Serious illness of family member   ———   ———

Financial

32. A major purchase or mortgage loan   ———   ———
33. A major business reversal or financial loss   ———   ———
34. A major change in finances (increased or decreased income, credit difficulties)   ———   ———

Personal and Social

35. A major personal achievement   ———   ———
36. A change in personal habits (dress, life-style, friends, etc.)   ———   ———
37. Sexual difficulties   ———   ———
38. Beginning or ceasing school or college   ———   ———
39. A vacation   ———   ———
40. Change in religious beliefs   ———   ———
41. Change in social activities   ———   ———
42. Legal difficulties   ———   ———
43. Change in political beliefs   ———   ———
44. A new, close personal relationship   ———   ———
45. A "falling out" in a close personal relationship   ———   ———

	Event Occurred	Your Adj. Score
46. Girlfriend or boyfriend problems	_____	_____
47. Loss, theft, or damage of personal property	_____	_____
48. An accident	_____	_____
49. A major decision regarding your immediate future	_____	_____

Everyone adapts to recent life changes differently. For example, some of us find that the adjustment to a new home is enormous, while others say very little adjustment is necessary. Now "score" each of the life changes you checked as to the amount of personal adjustment it required.

Under "Your Adjustment Score" rate each occurrence from 1 to 100. For example, if you moved and felt it required very little adjustment, choose a low number. On the other hand, if you moved and it required considerable adjustment, select a higher score. For most people the degree of adjustment for a major life change such as marriage is estimated to be around 50, while a major life trauma such as death of a spouse might be close to 100. Rate each of your recent changes and get a total score: _____.

However, while everyone feels pain and stress upon a loss, after a period of time a person must recommit to life and engage the problems that he or she is left with. One must raise the children, find a new relationship or set of friends, build a new house, or look for a new job. Illness, chronic stress symptoms, depression, alcoholism, and other difficulties are associated not with loss in itself, but with a certain attitude toward losses that are themselves natural and inevitable. Everyone faces losses, some more than others. However, after the grieving period, a person whose attitude is that he can never really feel good and alive again, that life no longer has meaning, is at particular risk. This attitude, labeled the "helpless/hopeless" response to loss, is connected to illness and burnout. When a person expects the worst and never allows himself to recover, it is as if the body takes a cue from this attitude and it too gives up, causing the person to develop all manner of ailments that a hearty body could reject.

There will be more about this later in the chapter and in the next chapter. But the important point here is that it is not simply the loss and adjustment to a new world that are stressful, but our attitude and style of responding to the loss.

Thinking: The Human Way of Creating Stress

Our minds can increase or decrease the amount of pressure that an incident produces within us. During childhood each person develops certain areas of sensitivity. Our family and education lead us to look at the world in a certain way. We develop expectations and beliefs about other people, about our self-worth and our own abilities, and about the nature of things. All of these affect what things we see as stressful, difficult, or manageable.

For example, suppose our boss gives us a task that is beyond our ability or training. One person might mention that and ask for help. She would not see the assignment as particularly overwhelming and so the incident wouldn't trigger a psychophysical stress response. Another person might assume that he was expected to know how to do it and that if he didn't accomplish it his job would be on the line. Furthermore, the person might assume that asking for help is an indicator of failure. This set of expectations would make the assignment of that task the trigger for an intense stress response. The pressure of these perhaps unwarranted assumptions adds to the difficulty. The stress lies more in the expectations and the meaning the person adds to the task than in the difficulty of the task itself. This is the case with most of the incidents and situations that people find stressful.

Our definition of situations as well as our expectations and beliefs color all of our experience of stress. We may have to face a co-worker with whom we have had difficulty in the past. A new task may upset our expectations for a peaceful day. We may feel that a glance or a remark means something about our role or status. In each case it is our mind that is creating the stress, not the situation.

The way we evaluate a situation, its importance, and our sense of our capacity to face it determine our response. We may avoid or give up on a task that we feel is beyond our ability, and create stress for ourselves due to our self-criticism and annoyance at not having done it. We may create a fight with someone because we evaluate a situation or remark as ominous or threatening. We may see all situations as invitations for competition, or see everyone else's activities as letting us down.

Managing stress involves exploration of the ways that we talk to ourselves, what we assume, the way we define situations, and our own evaluation of our experience. The environment creates demands, challenges, changes, and pressures. Stress is a product of our interaction with our world; therefore we can change the amount of stress we are under by changing our way of seeing things and our responses to things.

Another way that our thinking can lead to burnout is by creating self-fulfilling prophecies. For example, a person who does not expect other people to help him may act distant, or may even tell himself that it doesn't pay to try. He never actually finds out that support is available because he assumes it is not. We make many assumptions about other people and about ourselves. We learned these expectations from our personal history, from our family, teachers, and our work life. Often we become so tied to certain types of expectations that we make them come true. Modifying negative beliefs and expectations about ourselves, our ability, and situations in the world is central to developing a sense of personal power.

So we see that before a situation can trigger the physiological stress response in our body, it must be filtered through our habitual ways of thinking about the world. Our psyche can decide that a minor daily hassle demands the total physical mobilization of the stress response, or it can decide that we can handle a difficult task with no sweat, and therefore not activate the total stress response.

We can think of our beliefs, thoughts, and feelings about things as a filtering or evaluating mechanism standing between the environment, with its pressures, changes, and stressors, and the activation of the psychophysiological stress response and/or an active coping response to meet the challenge.

Psychologist Albert Ellis calls this the A-B-C cycle of behavior. Event A takes place in our environment, which may or may not have something to do with us. There is our response, C, to that event. Between the two lies B, which is what we say to ourselves, how we see and define the situation, which in turn determines our response. We can define everything as our problem and burn ourselves out trying to do everything. Or we can tell ourselves that nothing we do will be good enough, which undermines our feeling about our response just enough to make us feel weak and powerless, usually even if we handle the situations effectively. Our perception of events, or our appraisal of situations, is a key determinant of our level of burnout or balance. In this section we explore the major types of self-defeating, even self-destructive, thought patterns that in themselves push us closer to burnout and keep us from mastering the world. Certain types of thinking place us in an unremitting world of overwhelming, even paralyzing, stress.

A	B	C
EVENT STRESSORS	PERCEPTUAL FILTERS	COPING RESPONSE
Pressures	Past experience	Psychophysical
Demands	Expectations	stress response
Changes	Evaluation	Burnout
Challenges	Beliefs	Coping response

Exercise 8 explores negative and critical thoughts about ourselves and about situations. None of the statements on the scale has a right or wrong answer. Rather, they illuminate the way we feel about ourselves and the things we expect from the world. From this scale you will have an idea about how positive or negative the conversations you have with yourself are.

Conversations with Ourselves. Most of the day, though we may be silent to people around us, we engage in a continual conversation with ourselves. Within our mind we listen to chatter about what we are doing. Sometimes we talk to ourselves about something about to happen. "I'm going to mess it up," "These things always turn out badly," "All the other guys at work are out to show me up," "My job is on the line with this project," "I just don't know how to do it," we may anticipate. Another person might have a different type of self-talk: "I can handle everything," "Things usually work out for the best," "The people at work like and respect me."

Negative and positive ways of talking to ourselves have a critical influence on our capacity to respond. The body triggers the stress response not only when something threatening is actually happening, but when we simply *think* about something threatening. So the person who is talking negatively to himself, worrying and thinking about all the bad things that might happen, is physically triggering the stress response within his body even before he confronts the actual event. Or if the event has already happened—say, a difficult project—thinking over and over about how badly you may have done also triggers the stress response not just once, but repeatedly until the body becomes exhausted. The results are headaches, gastric distress, diarrhea, and other stress symptoms, not so much due to a threatening *event*, but to the way we think about it over and over again.

There are many ways that we create negative and self-defeating conversations with ourselves.

Some of the more common forms of negative self-talk include:

Shoulds: As we choose not to do some things, or to follow other directions, we create stress by telling ourselves what we ought to be doing. We make demands on ourselves based on standards that are unrealistically high or impossible to fulfill.

Criticism: People may tell themselves they have not done well or have done something incorrectly. They are far more severe on themselves than others are.

Blame: People create stress by blaming themselves for situations that are either beyond their control or are perfectly reasonable.

Negative expectations: People create stress by imagining bad things that can happen, to which their bodies react

(text continues on page 55)

EXERCISE 8

SELF-ASSESSMENT: NEGATIVE THOUGHT PATTERNS

The following statements reflect some general attitudes and ways of thinking that can add to or create stress and frustration. Circle the number that reflects how strongly you agree or disagree, or how true or false they seem to be according to your own experience.

I. Self-Criticism and Self-Doubt	Strongly Agree	Agree	Disagree	Strongly Disagree
1. I am usually critical of my own performance	3	2	1	0
2. I make demands on myself that I wouldn't make on others	3	2	1	0
3. I never think what I do is good enough	3	2	1	0
4. I expect criticism from others for my work	3	2	1	0
5. I get very upset with myself when things don't work out the way I expected them to	3	2	1	0
6. When I am successful, I think I don't deserve it	3	2	1	0
7. I don't think much of myself	3	2	1	0
8. When something difficult arises, I find myself thinking of all the ways things can go poorly	3	2	1	0
9. I often find myself in unpleasant situations that I feel helpless to change	3	2	1	0
10. I often run into problems I can't solve	3	2	1	0
11. I don't feel that I have much control over the events in my life	3	2	1	0
12. When I am doing something, anxious and upsetting thoughts distract me	3	2	1	0

TOTAL

II. Negative Expectations	Strongly Agree	Agree	Disagree	Strongly Disagree
1. I find it hard to hope for the best	3	2	1	0
2. I expect the worst	3	2	1	0
3. Other people rarely seem to come through for me	3	2	1	0
4. I find it hard to look on the bright side of things	3	2	1	0
5. I am a naturally gloomy person	3	2	1	0
6. I have been continuously frustrated in my life by bad breaks	3	2	1	0
7. My life is empty and has no meaning	3	2	1	0
8. The future will probably not be as good as things are now	3	2	1	0
9. I often seem to get the raw end of the stick	3	2	1	0
10. Good fortune is mostly due to luck	3	2	1	0
11. When things aren't going my way, I usually feel it is useless to try to change them	3	2	1	0
12. Very little about life is fair or equitable	3	2	1	0
TOTAL				

A score of more than 10 on either part indicates that you have some serious negative attitudes, expectations, and beliefs about yourself that need to be changed.

as if the bad thing is actually taking place. Such worries can also create negative responses to actual situations.

Wrong assumptions: If a person links an event with a wrong conclusion, the event or response may take on unreasonable significance. Thus, thinking that people dislike you adds to your stress, and also affects your own behavior.

Can'ts: When we are afraid of a challenge or we doubt ourselves, or perhaps we do not want to do something, we do not look closely at our motivations. Instead we say that we cannot do something. This creates stress by placing a defect within ourselves, rather than exploring the perhaps good reasons to have doubts, fears, or simply not to do something.

Errors of Thinking. According to cognitive psychologists common difficulties such as depression, anxiety, and stress arise from illogical conclusions that people draw from the events that affect them. These thinking errors can be corrected through careful observation and practice.

Psychiatrist David Burns has adapted the cognitive therapy method pioneered by Beck and Ellis. He lists the most common distortions of thought.

All-or-nothing thinking: Seeing things in black-or-white categories. Any performance short of perfection is a total failure.

Overgeneralization: Seeing one negative event as a never-ending pattern of defeat.

Mental filter: Picking out a single negative detail and dwelling on it exclusively so your vision of everything becomes darkened.

Disqualifying the positive: Rejecting positive experiences by insisting they "don't count."

Jumping to conclusions: Formulating negative interpretations without sufficient evidence. This may involve misreading other people's minds or predicting negative outcomes for yourself.

Magnification (catastrophizing) or minimization: Exaggerating the importance of errors or problems, or inappropriately belittling the significance of your own assets.

Emotional reasoning: Assuming that your own negative emotions necessarily reflect the way things really are.

"Should" statements: Trying to motivate yourself to improve with "shoulds" and "shouldn'ts," as though you were

a delinquent child requiring punishment in order to accomplish anything.

Labeling: An extreme form of overgeneralization; instead of saying "I made a mistake," the person attaches a negative label, i.e., "I'm a loser."

Personalization: Blaming yourself inappropriately as the cause of a negative event.

Reflect on the things that you say about an event just after something difficult or stressful takes place. Think about the conclusions you draw about the world, and about yourself, and reflect upon how realistic and helpful it is for you to come to such conclusions. Many of the above distortions are simply methods of blaming oneself and making oneself helpless to do anything differently. By becoming aware that difficulties may be due to your thoughts and conclusions, you empower yourself to change these thoughts the next time something difficult happens in your life.

Exploring Your Definition of Stressful Situations. Look again at your Personal Stress Log. Use this to complete Exercise 9. This time reflect on the things that you said to yourself before, during, and after the event. Before, what was your frame of mind? Were you angry at yourself, or were you expecting the worst? Some people, for example, spend their lives either being sick or expecting to get sick. Others have a set of assumptions about people: they never come through, they don't like me. When they interact with co-workers, they see the situations only as confirming their worst fears.

In any stressful event we make many assumptions about what is happening, what other people mean, want, and feel, what needs to be done, and what it means to us. These are not aspects of the situation itself, but rather are part of our reading of it. These assumptions color our perception and determine the value we place on things. Look at some of the stressful events listed in your log, and write down what you assumed and said to yourself at each stage of the situation. Can you see how your assumptions and thoughts contributed to the event's stressfulness?

Even after a stressful event is over, it continues for us in the form of our thoughts and evaluations of what took place. If we feel that we were deprived of our self-esteem or lost face, for example, we may feel chagrined. Yet the other person may not have the same assessment, and a perceived disadvantage or conflict may exist largely inside ourselves. You will begin to see, as you conduct such reflection for each of the stressful events in your log, how much stress you cause yourself via your thoughts, assumptions, and evaluations.

The Inner Critic.   Our culture respects and rewards achievement and individual excellence, especially in men. From infancy we are compared with others and urged to do better. Teachers, parents, and peers often have high expectations of us. Many of us grow up feeling pressured, feeling that we have not achieved enough success, or trying to achieve unrealistically high goals.

There are many unintended, negative consequences to the drive to achieve and excel. First, we may have such high goals that nothing feels like success. We may not allow ourselves to enjoy or rest at any plateau or savor any achievement because we are too busy pushing ourselves for more. Another consequence is a secret feeling of unworthiness, of having failed. We may feel we have failed if we are not number one, or if we do not come up to our parents' expectations or their actual achievements. Yet another negative consequence is the growing feeling that people value us not for who we are, but for what we do. Many people feel estranged from what they have done, or distant from their achievements.

Too often a person grows up with an inner voice that is severely critical or doubting of her abilities. The inner critic is the voice of parents and teachers, sometimes talking to us in far harsher terms than any of the actual people in our life really do. The inner critic takes away any feeling of success and keeps us under relentless, unyielding pressure.

Think about the way you relate to yourself. Do you have a severe inner critic that expects the impossible or unattainable and doesn't let you rest? Write down some of the ways that you continually, and unconstructively, criticize yourself. For many, sadly, this is a long list.

Now look at the list of ways that your critic puts you down. Try to evaluate each criticism objectively. Look at what you have done and how well you perform tasks. Determine if your critic is useful, making suggestions for things you need to improve, or simply adding to your pressure and decreasing your ability to relax and feel good about your life.

Becoming aware of the extent to which your inner critic runs your life is an important part of changing. As you look at how you criticize yourself, you can see that your critic is not really you, it is the voice of other people. Perhaps you can begin to counter the negative thinking of your critic. Or you can begin to substitute positive statements, supportive and affirmative evaluations of your work.

Modifying Negative Thought Patterns.   You can change self-defeating or negative patterns by using several common techniques:

Check and modify assumptions. If you feel that your job is on the line, or that people don't really like you, or as you become aware of other self-defeating assumptions that you bring to situations, devise a way to clarify the actual situation. Often checking with other people

(text continues on page 59)

E X E R C I S E 9

MENTAL RESPONSES TO STRESSFUL SITUATIONS

List the four most persistent stressful situations that occur in your life:

1.

2.

3.

4.

For each situation list the things you assume, tell yourself, and expect:

1.

2.

3.

4.

For each of the stressful situations write down some of the things you expect from yourself, criticize yourself for, or negative things that you assume about yourself:

1.

2.

3.

4.

Finally, for each stressful situation write down some new things that you might assume about yourself and the situation, things that are more positive. What might you say to yourself the next time?

1.

2.

3.

4.

or simply realizing that your assumptions are unrealistic or extravagant can relieve stress.

Relax and tell yourself the opposite. When you see yourself saying negative things to yourself, worrying, or anticipating the worst, you can relax yourself (since the thoughts are probably making you tense) and then begin to imagine more positive situations, or say more complimentary things.

Use affirmations. People don't compliment other people, or themselves, as much as they might. Often we are critical of ourselves and forget all our positive qualities. When you find yourself being self-critical, write down a list of positive things about yourself, and things that you would like to happen. Place the list where you can read it often, on the refrigerator or bathroom mirror perhaps, and try to repeat these affirmative messages to yourself several times a day.

Positive Thinking

We can enhance the degree of control that we feel over our lives when we learn to modify some of the ways that we talk to ourselves and think about things. Many of the popular books on psychology, motivation, and self-care, from Dale Carnegie's pioneering *How to Win Friends and Influence People* and Norman Vincent Peale's *Power of Positive Thinking,* to the modern advice of Wayne Dyer, suggest that many of the difficulties in our lives stem from a lack of self-affirmation.

It is easy to dismiss such positive conversations and changes in our beliefs as evasions of our real problems. Nonetheless, the authors' experience is that people who begin consciously to modify their inner conversations and assumptions report an almost immediate improvement in their performance. Their energy increases and things seem to go better. It's all in their imagination, cynics say, and the authors hasten to agree. Of course it is, but so was the pressure they were under to begin with.

We live in a world where it is commonplace to blame others for our shortcomings, where negative messages about our own powers and worth are common. The unintended messages we often get from our parents, our teachers, and our employers are that we are not competent or not good. We take these messages into ourselves and repeat them until they become reality for us. We become powerless, incompetent, and incapable of responding to things, thereby giving up our sense of power.

Affirmations. Affirmations are positive personal statements that modify negative personal beliefs and expectations, and motivate and influence us in new directions. In a mechanistic sense, they are new programs that attempt to influence and change the dysfunctional attitudes and expectations that lead to negative results in our life. An affirmation is a positive statement about ourself and our potential that becomes true if we repeat it often enough—it becomes our internal reality. An affirmation takes effect when our behavior and feelings begin to flow from it.

Affirmations can be more or less effective. For example, just repeating to yourself "I will make a million dollars," is unlikely to be effective. Certain rules govern affirmations, and you can apply them to yourself to guide your personal change process. Affirmations are not attempts to apply magic to the external world, nor do they create the impossible (although impossibility is only a belief we hold about things); affirmations are rather an attempt to modify patterns of thought and belief that limit and frustrate us. Before you begin to create a set of affirmations for yourself, examine your negative patterns of thought, beliefs, and expectations. You have already discovered many ways that your mind-sets and conversations create unnecessary limits and keep you from coping successfully with the pressure of your life.

Use these rules to make your affirmations effective:

1. Place yourself in a receptive state of mind. Place yourself in a state of deep relaxation (as detailed in chapter 7), or simply take a few moments to get your body and psyche ready to receive new information. Before you begin, you need to tell yourself you are ready.

2. Make your affirmations short, clear, unambiguous, and specific. Break down complex desires and changes into smaller, simpler directives.

3. Phrase affirmations in the present tense. You are creating them as a psychic reality that will exist from the moment you state them to yourself.

4. Phrase them positively, as what you want to do. Avoid negative words like "stop," "not," or "don't." State what you actually want to think, feel, and do instead.

5. When you repeat your intentions, try to suspend your doubts, and inhibit a tendency to make a negative or doubting commentary. Do not undercut or undermine your affirmations. If you begin to think negatively, say "no" or "stop" to yourself, and continue the affirmation.

6. You should feel positive, expansive, and supportive as you say them.

7. Write down your sets of affirmations and place the list where you will see it repeatedly during the day. You need to keep reminding yourself of them to make them concrete and real for you.

8. Make affirmations a continuing, ongoing part of your life.

Now write a short beginning set of affirmations that will modify some of the negative things you think to yourself. Create affirmations concerning some of the important areas of your life. Let your affirmations be expansive and enabling. For example, you might create affirmations such as:

- I am healthy and full of well-being
- My work is meaningful and exciting to me
- I deserve to be loved and to have the love I desire in my life
- It's okay to get what I want
- I will let myself enjoy receiving from people who care about me
- I will let go of my anger
- I can accept my feelings as an important part of myself
- I can get what I want from other people
- My work supports my creativity and initiative

With these examples you should be able to come up with a list of affirmations in areas that are meaningful and important to you.

Spend a few moments several times a day slowly repeating your affirmations to yourself. As you repeat them, try to imagine how that affirmation is—or can be—true in your life; you might imagine the affirmation as it comes to be part of your life. Actually see yourself changing. Especially in moments of stress or pressure, affirmations will be useful reminders of your potential for change and your commitment to new ways of being.

CHAPTER 3

Empowerment: Responding Creatively to Life's Demands

The connection between heart disease and the behavior of the hard-driving, easily frustrated, always overwhelmed executive has settled into the popular imagination. The moral of the story is that we connect heart attacks and high blood pressure with the feeling of pushing ourselves too hard, or being overwhelmed by time pressures and demands. "Take it easy" becomes the formula for coping with stress. This advice is hard for most people to put into action; it is also only part of the story.

Suzanne Kobasa, a health researcher at the University of Chicago, felt this conclusion was incomplete. After all, she and many of her colleagues and friends had high energy, worked hard, met a variety of pressing life-demands, and did not have heart disease. Why, she asked, do some people remain healthy in high-stress environments (and who of us does not live in one?) and others succumb to burnout and various stress-related ailments? The preliminary results of her research offer a glimpse of how our personal *style* of meeting demands may be more important than how many stressors there are, or what kind.

Kobasa surveyed healthy executives in high-stress occupations. They saw their work lives differently than another group of high-pressure executives who experienced more than their share of illnesses, burnout, and stress-related difficulties. First, while the healthy group was not really any more in control than their distressed peers, they *felt* they were in control of the things that mattered to them. Obviously their sense of control was more than simply the raw power to get things done. (We explore this difference in the rest of this chapter.) Two other distinguishing characteristics of the healthy executives

were a greater feeling of involvement in whatever they were doing, and a desire to seek challenges, take risks, and look for new
slants.

To many people personal power means making other people do
what we want them to do and having demands come in a predictable
sequence so that we can meet them with our planned and anticipated
response. Being in control lasts as long as we can make the outside
world submit to our will, and as long as it does not surprise us. If the
world doesn't play by our rules, we feel our control slipping away.

But in the authors' work, and from our reading of research on
health and management of stress, a different version of personal power
emerges. Personal power comes not from making the world predictable, but from a sense of confidence that we can meet whatever demands come up creatively and effectively. This means that we know
our limits, and limit our expectations, as well as utilizing our skills and
strengths. The sense of power that Kobasa's healthy executives ex-
hibited is a sense of self-reliance combined with a knowledge that
they had a set of skills that enabled them to manage even unpredictable, frustrating, or slightly overwhelming events.

This sense of control is more than a feeling, or a personality state.
It can be broken down into its essential elements, and a person can
begin to discover ways to enhance it. We will focus on the major
components of this sense of personal power—the way we respond to
stressful situations and our general style of coping with them. We need
to create a world and a sense of ourselves that includes possibilities
for our making things different. This chapter explores coping styles
that enhance control and actively resolve situations, and also those
which avoid or make things worse.

Each of us has learned a style of relating to demands that sometimes stands us in good stead, protects our health, and ensures our
success. At other times our style adds to our difficulty and causes us
trouble and pain. First you will explore your common patterns of responding to stress, your "stress signature." Then you will consider,
imagine, and practice new responses to stressful situations. Finally,
the authors will offer a style of active coping that optimizes health and
personal power.

Demands are not presented to us. We choose which ones to take
on, and how we see them. Then we determine the nature of our response, which can resolve or alleviate a demand or make it worse. We
can respond defensively, to protect ourselves and our psyche, rather
than responding offensively to the demand itself. Overall, we have
certain basic approaches to most situations, which make up our personal style, our personality. The way we respond to demands is called
"coping," and our way of coping is responsible for our health, our
illness, the buildup of negative stress within our bodies and psyches,
and the degree of burnout or balance we experience in our lives.

EMPOWERMENT AND CONTROL

Burnout can be seen as a failure of self-regulation. It is neither a necessary nor a predictable effect of certain life crises. Burnout sets in when we do not respond directly to demands, or when we overreact or misplace our reaction to events. This behavior then continues over time despite the lack of positive results. As we have seen, burnout breeds within an environment where the individual feels a sense of helplessness to respond to demands and a sense of hopelessness about the future. "I'm not free, I'm not able to make a difference," a person who is moving toward burnout says to herself. As the authors have suggested, this belief or expectation then becomes true simply because the person acts as if it is true.

At the opposite extreme is a person who feels empowered to make a difference in his actions. Her power is neither absolute nor infallible; the world still has the power to defeat, frustrate, or deprive her of what she wants. But the person who feels a sense of power always knows she has the capacity to make a next move, to choose a meaningful response to whatever situation is presented to her. Her choices are not arbitrary, but arise out of a sense of her needs, values, and goals; they support her sense of self and respect the realities and regularities of this life. Nonetheless, this response can also be creative, playful, and novel, not formalized and limited by past precedents. The person is not a victim of life, but rather has the capacity to be self-determining, self-organizing, and creative in response to demands.

The capacity for creative responses is what differentiates the person from the robot or the computer. We always can learn, adapt, and grow. To a degree we can let go of the past. The exploration of the basis of our sense of personal power and its elements keeps telling us that no matter what demands are placed upon us, we can come up with a creative response. Creative responses begin within the individual, in the way he or she organizes reality and reads situations. Human beings are unique in their capacity to anticipate and plan—to create their future—to explore alternatives within themselves, and to evaluate the results and make changes, even in mid-action.

What does a person see? Does he see opportunities or only missed chances? How well does a person acknowledge her own capacities and skills? Does she maximize or minimize them? In what ways does a person distort situations or read them clearly? These questions can be approached not by a study of the pressures and demands that fall upon us, but by looking at the way we organize our inner worlds and the way we visualize ourselves and our abilities.

Meaningful Control

People who handle the stress of their lives well feel in control of their world. That does not mean that they have total control over everything or everyone around them—indeed, studies of those rare individuals who had such total control show that they were anxious and fearful—but rather that they feel they can do something about the things that distress them. There is something that they can do, and they select projects that allow them to succeed. When faced with a stressful situation, they pick the aspect of the situation that they can do something about. We use the term "optimal control:" people who manage stress well seem to be in control of their immediate environment.

Some people feel that they can control nothing, that they are victims of their environment and circumstances. They don't even try to make their lives better. They suffer from undercontrol, or what has been termed the "helpless/hopeless syndrome." These people are depressed and suffer from a variety of stress-related health and emotional problems. At the opposite extreme are those people who take on every project and have to do everything themselves. They find it hard to trust people, who always let them down. These people suffer from overcontrol, which has been associated with what has been termed the "Type A behavior syndrome." Overcontrol, too, is associated with health and stress-related difficulties.

We can make a diagram of these three possibilities:

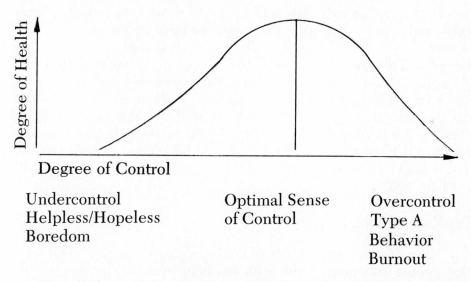

One of the primary qualities of effective stress management is the sense of control we have over our world. We have this sense of control when we know how to choose situations we can do something about and thereby regularly accomplish clearcut goals and experience success and relaxation. The helpless/hopeless person can never experience success or a sense of accomplishment; neither can a Type A person, because he never feels safe, secure, or finished, since there is always another task to be done. People at both extremes are never at rest or comfortable.

How do you approach life? Do you tend to see yourself as a victim or as a martyr? Do you recognize your limits and respect them? Do you select goals and projects, or tend to take on everything that comes your way, as if you have to? At which extreme of this polarity do you live, and what can you do to bring yourself to the optimal, balance point?

Assessing and Modifying Your Coping Style

Our response to each day's demands, crises, and challenges depends on the situation, as well as on our personal bag of tricks. We have developed certain preferred, comfortable ways to manage difficulty, to approach tasks, and to respond to crises. These are our coping strategies, and they work for us. Some of us have only a few of them and respond the same rigid way no matter what the situation. Others have many responses and fit them flexibly to the task. The self-assessment exercises in this section will help you continue to explore the different ways that you respond to stressful situations.

In Chapter 2 you kept a Personal Stress Log. If you go back and review the log, you will probably recognize recurring patterns and chronic problem areas.

You will continue to learn about your responses to difficult situations, your coping style. You will be asked about your thoughts, emotions, and actions that make up several positive and negative aspects of coping. This will help you evaluate how well your own style works for you and the specific areas where you need to initiate change. These changes will allow you to seize more effective control over your world.

Your coping style is not all positive or all negative. It contains many elements, some of which are helpful in some situations, and others that might be needed in different circumstances. After you have completed Exercises 10 and 11, you will have a list of your positive and negative coping responses, and know what causes the most difficulty for you.

Profiles of Coping Styles

The self-assessment scales of coping styles relate to several ways that people commonly cope with stressful events. The first six are coping difficulties, styles of managing stress that in most situations are more dysfunctional than effective. The final three styles of coping seem to be helpful in managing stress and in taking care of the person. Now that you have some idea of your characteristic styles of response, here are descriptions of each dysfunctional style and some ways to make changes.

Withdrawal.   Withdrawal is a style of avoiding, fearing, or otherwise putting off action that would reduce the pressure. In this style a

E X E R C I S E 10

SELF-ASSESSMENT: COPING DIFFICULTIES

Certain common methods of coping with stressful situations clearly lead to difficulty when overused. Each of the statements below corresponds to common coping methods. Circle the number that most closely corresponds to how frequently you act that way in stressful situations. Then total your scores for each coping difficulty.

I. Withdrawal	Often	Sometimes	Rarely	Never
1. I avoid challenges or new situations	3	2	1	0
2. I am cautious and shy away from risks	3	2	1	0
3. I try to forget difficult tasks facing me	3	2	1	0
4. I find it hard to plan ahead and anticipate difficulties	3	2	1	0
5. I find it hard to get involved in what I am doing	3	2	1	0
6. I find minor tasks to avoid facing major ones	3	2	1	0
7. I forget things I have to do	3	2	1	0
8. I don't let myself get emotionally involved in things	3	2	1	0
9. I fall asleep when things are difficult	3	2	1	0
TOTAL I				

II. Helplessness	Often	Sometimes	Rarely	Never
1. Most of my stress seems to be unpredictable	3	2	1	0
2. No matter how hard I try, I can't accomplish what I want	3	2	1	0
3. I am not able to give what I want to those close to me	3	2	1	0
4. I often find myself in situations that I feel helpless to do anything about	3	2	1	0
5. I often run into problems that I can't solve	3	2	1	0
TOTAL II				

III. Internalizing				
1. I keep my feelings to myself	3	2	1	0
2. When I'm upset I tend to hold it in and suffer silently	3	2	1	0
3. I don't let anyone know I am under pressure	3	2	1	0
4. I try to brace myself against pressure and stress	3	2	1	0
5. I don't like to disagree with people	3	2	1	0
6. When I'm upset I avoid other people and go off alone	3	2	1	0
7. I hold in my anger and frustration	3	2	1	0
TOTAL III				

IV. Emotional Outbursts	Often	Sometimes	Rarely	Never
1. When I'm upset I blame someone else for things	3	2	1	0
2. I blow up and let off steam	3	2	1	0
3. I find that I easily become irritable	3	2	1	0
4. I cry or fall apart emotionally and lose control	3	2	1	0
5. I find myself angry	3	2	1	0
TOTAL IV				

V. Overcontrolling

	Often	Sometimes	Rarely	Never
1. I try never to be late for appointments	3	2	1	0
2. I am rushed	3	2	1	0
3. I get impatient when I have to wait	3	2	1	0
4. I try to do everything myself	3	2	1	0
5. I don't have time for hobbies or outside interests	3	2	1	0
6. I worry about things before I do them	3	2	1	0
7. I rarely take time for myself	3	2	1	0
8. I always put other people before myself	3	2	1	0
9. Other people let me down	3	2	1	0
10. I don't get much satisfaction from my achievements	3	2	1	0
11. There is never enough time to get things done	3	2	1	0
12. I can't start a project without thinking of another one facing me	3	2	1	0
TOTAL V				

VI. Type A Behavior	Often	Sometimes	Rarely	Never
1. I try to be on time for all appointments	3	2	1	0
2. I find it hard to find time for personal errands	3	2	1	0
3. I am faced with irritating and frustrating situations	3	2	1	0
4. I eat rapidly and finish meals before other people	3	2	1	0
5. I find myself doing several things at one time	3	2	1	0
6. I give everything I have to my work	3	2	1	0
7. I like to be the best at whatever I do	3	2	1	0
8. I get impatient when someone is taking too long at a job I could do more quickly	3	2	1	0
9. I tend to keep my feelings to myself	3	2	1	0
10. I am very ambitious	3	2	1	0
11. I have few interests outside of work	3	2	1	0
12. I want my worth to be recognized by the people around me	3	2	1	0
13. I hurry even when I have plenty of time	3	2	1	0
14. I set deadlines for myself	3	2	1	0
15. When I am tired, I tend to keep pushing myself to finish a task	3	2	1	0
16. I am hard-driving and competitive	3	2	1	0
17. I am precise about details	3	2	1	0
18. I think ahead to the next task	3	2	1	0
19. I tend to get angry when I am in situations beyond my control	3	2	1	0
20. I let other people set standards for me	3	2	1	0
TOTAL VI				

SELF-ASSESSMENT: ACTIVE COPING

Accounts of successful coping with stress emphasize certain qualities. This exercise assesses the degree to which you utilize active coping strategies. For each statement circle the number indicating how frequently you employ that type of behavior when confronted with a problem.

I. Support Seeking	Often	Sometimes	Rarely	Never
1. Find someone to delegate it to	3	2	1	0
2. Share it with someone	3	2	1	0
3. Talk to others about it and share feelings	3	2	1	0
4. Seek information from others	3	2	1	0
5. Try to find someone who knows how to handle it	3	2	1	0
6. Talk it over with someone you trust	3	2	1	0
7. Seek advice and support of friends	3	2	1	0
8. Talk problem over with counselor or doctor	3	2	1	0
9. Share it with the family	3	2	1	0
TOTAL I				

II. Diversion/Tension Release	Often	Sometimes	Rarely	Never
1. Decide it's not worth worrying about	3	2	1	0
2. Do relaxation exercises	3	2	1	0
3. Do active physical exercises	3	2	1	0
4. Look at the humorous side of it	3	2	1	0
5. Go away for a while to get perspective	3	2	1	0
6. Reward or indulge yourself when finished	3	2	1	0
7. Decide it's not really your problem	3	2	1	0
TOTAL II				

III. Direct Action	Often	Sometimes	Rarely	Never
1. Take extra care to do a good job	3	2	1	0
2. Finish the job immediately	3	2	1	0
3. Do as good a job as possible under the circumstances	3	2	1	0
4. Think it through and try to change your viewpoint or way of looking at the situation	3	2	1	0
5. Put it in its place, don't let it overwhelm you	3	2	1	0
6. Anticipate and plan ahead to meet challenges	3	2	1	0
7. Make several alternate plans	3	2	1	0
8. Let people know about angry or uncomfortable feelings	3	2	1	0

III. Direct Action (continued)	Often	Sometimes	Rarely	Never
9. Let people know the task is too much or you are too busy	3	2	1	0
10. Negotiate so that the task is more manageable	3	2	1	0
TOTAL III				

You have explored positive and negative aspects of your coping style. To evaluate your overall pattern of coping, indicate in the first list below which responses are a problem for you. Next, enter your scores for positive coping assets. You now have a sense of your coping style, with its positive and negative aspects. You may end up with just one or two problem areas, or a greater number of assets and liabilities.

Coping Style	Danger Zone	Your Score	A Problem for You?
Dysfunctional Styles:			
I. Withdrawal	12–27	_____	_____
II. Helplessness	8–15	_____	_____
III. Internalizing	10–21	_____	_____
IV. Emotional Outbursts	8–15	_____	_____
V. Overcontrolling	15–39	_____	_____
VI. Type A Behavior	20–60	_____	_____
Helpful Styles:			
I. Support Seeking	1–12	_____	_____
II. Diversion/Tension Release	1–10	_____	_____
III. Direct Action	1–12	_____	_____

person maintains the level of stress he is under by not doing something about it. He may be afraid to do what is needed, or he may have all sorts of reasons and rationalizations for what he is not doing. But the fact remains that the source of pressure does not go away. There are all sorts of psychological theories about why people engage in this seemingly dysfunctional pattern. They may be afraid to succeed or they may lack self-confidence. They may have simply gotten into the habit of not acting, or they may not be able to imagine how good it would feel to get things done. They may fear change and risk and wish for things to remain the way they were in the past. The reasons are less important than learning a way to motivate oneself to action.

If you score high on withdrawal, you are not taking risks, allowing yourself to make changes, completing important tasks, and meeting responsibilities. This in turn leads to worry, frustration, fear, and depression. There are several ways to begin to change.

1. Make a list of important tasks, personal priorities, and major demands on you. Next list all the good personal reasons that you have for not doing them. You will find that you have many fears, emotional complications, and other difficulties that prevent you from tackling tasks. These may include fearing further tasks that will begin when you finish one, resenting or having difficulty with the person asking you to do it, not wanting or feeling right about the task, or feeling that someone else should have that job or help you with it. Now think of some ways to change your reasons for not doing the task. Set a deadline for yourself and try to face the task directly.

2. Take some time and get yourself into a state of quiet relaxation. Slowly, in your mind's eye, imagine yourself doing the task. Imagine it in as minute detail as you can, step by step. Try to let your body feel what doing the task is like. Imagine that you are doing the task well and feeling good about it. When you see yourself completing the task, imagine how good you will feel, and the rewards and benefits you will receive from others. Do this exercise several times, over several days.

3. Create rewards for yourself. At each step of a complicated task—and when you are finished—give yourself a special reward that feels good to you. Also, be alert to the responses of others to your activity as another sort of reward—a boost in your self-esteem.

4. Think about the little things that you want, or would like to do, things like asking someone for a date, trying something new, exposing your feelings, or asserting your

rights. Each day try to take a risk or two, and watch your own response and how others respond to your initiative.

5. If you find it especially difficult to begin to do something, sit for a few moments and ask yourself why you won't do the task. It may help to imagine what you are afraid of, or to imagine the worst thing that can happen. Then think about whether you really couldn't accept and live with that worst possible outcome. Then imagine the best possible outcome. If you continue to feel a deep inner resistance, the task is probably something that you simply shouldn't do and you should tell the person who expects it of you that you will not complete the task and some of the reasons why. Some assignments and obligations do not have to be carried out, and your resistance is telling you this.

Helplessness.   Helplessness is not a fact, it is a way of experiencing oneself. Helplessness is the sense that you cannot do things or that what you can do won't make a difference. Helplessness is usually paired with hopelessness, and this whole style is an extreme form of withdrawal. When demands or needs are experienced, the person freezes and hides. As a consequence the person never gets what she wants, never experiences any sense of personal power or ability, so the feeling is amplified over time until it becomes depression and giving up. Nothing is worth doing. They experience themselves as helpless, as victims. The person does not even try to resist or overcome a source of stress, and it seems that the body, like the psyche, gives up and illness begins to take root.

Helplessness is a self-defeating cycle: you perceive yourself as not having ability, therefore you don't get better at things or achieve success, which justifies and continues the process. Inactivity breeds inactivity. For this reason helpful approaches to the problem of helplessness—extreme withdrawal—aim at short-circuiting this self-defeating pattern.

The feeling of helplessness can be redefined as a problem stemming from saying negative things to oneself. Modifying helplessness begins by observing, and writing down, some of the negative things that you tell yourself about your ability, about the world, and about yourself. These self-statements serve to justify continued doing nothing. Look at your list and try to remove yourself and think about each statement objectively. Is it actually true from your experience, or was there perhaps only one or two events that led to your conclusion? Do something to test your assumption. For example, if you feel that nobody really cares about you and that is why you don't approach anyone or go out socially, you might call up some acquaintances and have a dinner party.

Another area to explore is the expectations and myths you have about your performance. Many people can't begin because they expect such unachievable perfection from themselves, or they are frustrated because they feel they "should" do so many things. Exploring the nature of your expectations and demands on yourself can lead you to revise them, which in turn frees you for action.

Another approach is to take direct action. People who feel chronic helplessness often say they don't want to do anything until they feel better. However, doing nothing does not make them feel better; it makes them feel worse. Therefore, when you feel helpless the solution is to do things that you don't expect to be helpful, or that you don't think will bring you what you want, simply because your experience is that doing nothing makes you feel worse. Do *anything*, and see how you feel afterward. If you begin to do little things, despite your negative feelings, you'll begin to perk up and experience rewards from what you do. This in turn leads to more activity, and the spiral is reversed to a positive direction.

Internalizing.   If you fill a balloon with air, eventually it bursts. Similarly, when a person tries to hold in more and more feelings, handle intolerable amounts of pressure, and do things on his own, the pressure mounts up. Frustration, resentment, and psychophysiological arousal build up and he never gets an opportunity to relax and go back to baseline, to release the stress. He is left after each accomplishment with a residue of unrelieved stress, which takes root in the form of any of the stress symptoms listed earlier.

Internalizers keep things to themselves. They feel that telling others how they feel is beside the point, sometimes even downright dangerous. They may fear conflict, or rationalize that sharing feelings is unproductive. They keep their pressure to themselves and rarely ask for help. Other people may see them as paragons of calmness and poise, and that is their intention. Unfortunately, an internalizer is often asked to do more and more, because of his nature, and another sort of self-defeating spiral is generated. Internalizing is common because the model of male behavior in our culture includes keeping cool under pressure and not sharing feelings. But there are definite health consequences and costs to internalizing, just as there are self-defeating long-term consequences of the Type A style, which our culture also values. While internalizing is useful in some crisis situations, it is isolating and creates undue tension and unreleased stress.

The opposite of keeping feelings in is letting them out. Letting out feelings has been caricatured as the self-centered, boorish outburst of emotions, typified in primal screaming. Yet effective expression of feelings does demand consideration of the situation and the person addressed. Feelings can be expressed flamboyantly or quietly, with similar sense of release inside yourself. To modify internalizing behavior you need to be more aware of feelings as they are building up, and then find appropriate pathways to express them.

Most internalizers have the experience of suddenly becoming aware of an almost intolerable buildup of frustration, anger, or stress symptoms, such as a headache. They have not been paying attention to their body; all of their attention was trained on their environment, their outer world. Change this tendency by practicing the body awareness exercises outlined in Chapter 7. Check in with yourself as you are working and as you begin to experience stress. Note what feelings are building up, how you feel about things. Sometimes just being aware of your feelings, without necessarily expressing them to other people, is enough to help you take steps to change the situation.

Another pathway is to explore your reasons for holding your feelings in. Think of some situations where you did not tell co-workers or family members what you were feeling. It is interesting to note that people who hold feelings in usually hold in both positive *and* negative feelings. Write down some of your reasons for not sharing feelings. These may be fears of how people will react, anticipation of rejection, resistance or anger from others. They may stem from assumptions about yourself: a real man does not talk about feelings, he keeps such things to himself. When you explore your reasons, you may find they are less persuasive than you expected.

Separate expression of feelings from demands. Many people feel that when they express a feeling it is a demand for something from another person. If you express anger, for example, the person you express it to has an obligation to do something about it. That is one reason people fear other people's feelings and hold in their own: they fear or recoil from obligations. You can begin to express how you feel without having an expectation that the recipient ought to change as a result of it. Your feeling is important information about you that needs to be stated so that the people around you can know how you are reacting. Many fears and worries are created by speculating about other people's feelings. By gently letting people know how you feel, you will begin to see how many of your fears and negative expectations were groundless.

Emotional Outbursts.   Emotional outbursts are really the long-term outcome of internalizing, just as helplessness is the long-term outcome of withdrawal. When you hold feelings in, they build up. One of the ways to discharge feelings is to blow up, usually on a safer occasion than the situation where the feeling originally arose. For example, we are concerned about our own performance and instead get angry and make unfair demands on our subordinates. Or we are frustrated with our marital relationship and find ourselves blowing up at our children, rather than looking at the actual source of our feelings.

There are two primary purposes of emotional outbursts. First, they release tension in a safe environment. Second, they often involve shifting blame and responsibility. When we are frustrated or under stress, one self-defeating emotional response is to relieve ourselves of responsibility by blaming another person. This process often leads to the curious outcome of two people arguing about who is responsible for something, while neither person alone, or both together, does anything about the situation. Shifting the blame is one mode of avoidance of responsibility. The negative consequence of blowing up at or blaming another person is to shift one's own stress and frustration to that person. Blowing up acts like a hot potato—the tension is passed along to another person. But the source of the frustration is untouched.

Dealing with emotional blowouts is paradoxically similar to modifying internalizing. It includes becoming aware of emotions when they are being created, and discharging them in the appropriate situation. The person who finds herself blowing up needs to inquire into the origin of these frustrating feelings and find another way to express them. Instead of shifting responsibility for feelings to another person, the process of exploring feelings involves asking yourself why you feel that way. Then you can make changes in the situation that created the feeling, not make demands on or shift tension to other people.

Overcontrolling. Keeping things under control is one of the most important and successful methods of stress management. However, the difficulties many people experience in coping with stress, including those with Type A behavior, stem from trying to anticipate every reaction of other people, trying to control every situation, and trying to plan for every eventuality. At some arbitrary point keeping meaningful control over one's environment becomes trying to keep too much under one's control. This creates anxiety because it is impossible. Overcontrolling makes the world more stressful.

We try to keep things under control by accomplishing every task, meeting every obligation, and taking care of everything around us. Nothing can be put off or declined. This is tiring and frustrating, in many ways similar to Type A behavior.

Modifying a coping style that tends toward overcontrolling involves several elements. First, priorities and tasks need to be evaluated, and tasks that can be dropped, or for which help can be discovered, are modified. The section on time management later in this chapter offers useful suggestions to people who overcontrol their environment.

Second, moving away from controlling too much involves confronting the fear of not being in control. Why do we do all these things in our lives? Are we afraid to displease people around us, or disappoint them? Are we afraid of failure? Do we doubt our worth, or feel that we are unappreciated? If you have feelings like these, you are not likely to feel better simply by doing everything that is humanly possible. There will always be reason to fear others' opinion or your own abilities. Looking honestly at the feelings and attitudes that lie behind your behavior is the most effective way to make changes in dysfunctional coping strategies.

Type A Behavior. The most clearly established connection between a response to stress and health is the connection between what has been termed Type A behavior and all forms of coronary heart disease. Along with proper diet, regular exercise, and not smoking, the modification of this method of coping is one of the most important ways that a person can prevent illness, as well as prevent all sorts of minor stress symptoms.

Type A behavior, as defined by cardiologists Meyer Friedman and Ray Rosenman, and psychologists David Glass and C. D. Jenkins, is a blend of emotional responses and activity in response to the demands of life, especially in relation to work tasks. According to Rosenman and Friedman, Type A behavior is

> an action-emotion complex . . . [that] can be observed in any person who is aggressively involved in a chronic, incessant struggle to achieve more and more in less and less time, and, if required, to do so against the opposing efforts of other things or persons.
>
> [It is] exhibited by people who are unable—or unwilling—to evaluate their own competence. Such people prefer to judge themselves by the evaluations of those whom they believe are their superiors. And to enhance themselves in other people's eyes, they attempt to increase the quantity (but rarely the quality) of their achievements. Their self-esteem becomes increasingly dependent on the status they believe they achieve.
>
> Unfortunately, such people pay a price. Any degree of self-esteem which they gain in this manner is apparently not enough to allay the insecurity and consequent agitation engendered by their "surrender" to outside criteria, to the authority of others. . . .
>
> . . . This chronic and incessant struggle . . . together with a free-floating, but covert, and usually well-rationalized hostility make up the Type A Behavior pattern. The sense of urgency and hostility give rise to irritation, impatience, aggravation and anger.

The characteristic behavioral and physical indicators of Type A behavior are:

Time Urgency

- Facial tautness expressing tension and anxiety
- Knee jiggling or rapid tapping of fingers
- Rapid, frequently dysrhythmic speech that sometimes cuts off the final words of sentences
- Respiratory sighing

- Doing several things at once (e.g., dictates while driving, reads while using electric shaver)
- During conversation, also thinking about other matters, rarely giving the other person undivided attention
- Eats and walks fast, and does not like to dawdle at table after eating
- Finds it difficult to sit and do nothing

Hostility
- Facial set exhibiting aggression and hostility (eye and jaw muscles)
- Ticlike drawing back of corner of lips, almost exposing teeth
- Use of clenched fist and table pounding or excessively forceful use of hands and fingers
- Explosive, staccato, frequently unpleasant sounding voice
- Irritation and rage when asked about past events in which he became angered
- Easily aroused irritabilities if kept waiting for any reason or if driving behind a car moving too slowly
- General distrust of other people's motives, i.e., distrust of altruism
- Plays any type of game (even with his young children) to win

Friedman notes that Type A behavior may initially bring about career success and achievement, and some life satisfaction. But the negative consequences soon outweigh the gains. The Type A person has difficulty in working with others and in adjusting to change and the unexpected. The frustration builds as the person never achieves satisfaction or peace. In addition, over time the Type A person becomes more and more one-dimensional, as he or she gives up hobbies and leisure activities, and even limits involvement with family and friends. Often a traumatic event—breakup of a marriage, loss of a job, passed over for promotion, failure of an effort—can lead to a reevaluation of this style of coping.

The Type A behavior scale allows you to estimate the degree to which you exhibit this style of coping with stress. This pattern is extremely common—and indeed encouraged—within our culture, so don't be overly distressed if you discover you exhibit many of its qualities. The Type A behavior pattern can be modified. People can learn new ways to cope, and once they find these methods rewarding, and develop new habits, they are much more effective at coping with the stress of their lives.

Friedman's change program involves four components:

1. Reevaluating every one of your activities to trim their activity level way down. Learn time management and prioritizing.

2. Learn to recognize your hidden anger and hostility, rather than deny it, and learn new ways to handle anger openly.

3. Practice and drill daily in walking, eating, talking, and driving at a slower pace.

4. Learn how to pay attention to the here-and-now, and to react positively, even with pleasure, to situations that before would be frustrating.

Active Coping. People who feel they respond successfully to stressful situations have incorporated the three aspects of active coping into their behavior.

Support Seeking: We cannot live in the world alone, and many of the dysfunctional styles of coping—withdrawal, helplessness, internalizing, emotional outbursts, Type A behavior, overcontrolling—involve moving away from supportive relationships with other people. They involve not sharing feelings and tasks. Support seeking, as we will see, involves creating positive working relationships. It is perhaps the best insulation against the negative effects of stress.

Diversion/Tension Release: Taking care of your body and allowing regular activities to help release the tension that builds up during the day are crucial to effective coping with stress. Sometimes diversion can seem like avoidance but, like control, it is a matter of balance and whether one returns to the work task renewed and refreshed.

Direct Action: Eventually most tasks cannot be avoided. The more we take action to work on what is needed in our environment, the more we feel in control, and the more we eliminate the source of our stress.

Support seeking and diversion/tension release are discussed in Chapters 4 and 7. First we look at direct action.

Coping and Control

From research evidence as well as from the authors' own experience, the healthiest and most effective people have learned to achieve a balance between taking care of themselves—self-renewal—and taking on the challenges that are presented to them. These people optimize their sense of personal control, seek challenge, and are involved in their work. They select the challenges they will face or those they set as their personal goals, and they face them directly with a minimum of avoidance and evasion. However, they do not neglect the needs of their bodies or push themselves too far, and they do not always go it alone. They call on help and supportive resources from other people.

In this section we explore the qualities of active, positive styles of coping, and how to modify your personal style toward greater effectiveness. People have problems in coping when their responses to stressful situations do not get the desired result. They either over-respond, underrespond, or respond in the wrong place or direction. When we respond to situations automatically without reflection or planning, using habits learned years before, we rob ourselves of flexibility. Another kind of difficulty arises from acting out of an incomplete understanding of the effects of our actions, without considering the end result of our response. For example, one manager continually berated his subordinates, thinking that the work had to get done. But he never explored the possible effects of his angry outbursts on the behavior of his employees. The unintended consequence was that his subordinates began to withhold information and avoid him, diminishing everyone's effectiveness.

Action versus Self-support.   When we face a stressful situation, our efforts to cope can take two basic directions. First, we can respond directly to the situation itself, by doing something to diminish the pressure. But coping usually involves more than that. In the stress response our body becomes aroused physiologically, and we also have a strong emotional response. Whether we pay attention to them or not, stressful events arouse fears and angers. Our self-esteem or our well-being is threatened, and we often need to minister to an injured psyche. Thus, coping consists of handling a situation and also protecting and regenerating ourselves.

This double task is where the difficulties most often arise. Sometimes we cope with stress exclusively by handling the situation itself, without much attention to our emotional or psychological needs. Other coping responses focus primarily on self-protection, the preservation of our self-esteem, and do little to modify the external situation. Effective coping demands attention to both types of need.

When we look at the six dysfunctional coping styles—withdrawal, helplessness, internalizing, emotional outbursts, overcontrolling, and Type A behavior—we can begin to notice that the dysfunctional aspects of these responses lie in the way that they tend to protect the psyche more than they manage the demand.

Looking more closely, we see that withdrawal and helplessness are motivated by a feeling that we are not up to meeting the demand or accomplishing the task. Since we doubt ourselves, we pull back from the challenge. Naturally, the outcome supports our negative opinion of ourselves, since we do not change the situation that faces us. So we continue to feel bad about ourselves, and the pressure or demand continues to loom over us.

The next pair of dysfunctional responses get us in trouble because they are poor attempts to deal with the emotions produced by stressful situations. The internalizer keeps her feelings to herself, often not even being aware of them. She does not share feelings, needs, difficulties, or problems. The internalizer thus misses the chance to get help and emotional support from others. Many internalizers do not feel that other people care about them or their problems, and so they hold back. The person who has emotional outbursts experiences a variation of this same problem. He internalizes distress over a period of time until the pressure leads to an explosion. When it comes, it is out of proportion to the trigger event, and more often than not acts to push other people away, people who might otherwise be helpful resources. Thus people are bewildered by the emotional intensity, or they feel attacked.

The final two patterns have some similarities to each other. Overcontrolling, the opposite of the helpless or withdrawal response, tries to gain control over everything in the environment, including people. It rarely is effective because other people respond by resisting attempts to be controlled. The Type A behavior pattern joins overcontrol with overscheduling and an inability to tolerate frustration. Both of these responses may handle some demands effectively, but over time they tend to lead to exhaustion and burnout.

In contrast look at the active coping responses: support seeking, diversion/tension release, and direct action. Each of these copes with some part of the stressful situation. Seeking help and support is a way of sharing a burden and reflects the research finding that people work best when they work together. The second response is to take care of the body using the self-renewal methods that are described in later chapters. Direct action is the problem-solving part of the triad.

When you face a stressful situation, ask yourself these questions:

1. How do I manage or take care of the demand or pressure? Does my response leave the demand or pressure untouched, or do I do something about it? Of course, we cannot simply decide that a demand is not our problem. Many people reduce stress by realizing that many of the tasks they take on are really meant for colleagues, subordinates, or family members. But all coping must effectively do *something* about the source of a demand or it will be ineffective and lead to future stress.

2. How am I taking care of my emotional response to the pressure, and protecting my body and psyche? These self-care and self-renewal activities will be explored later. But in evaluating coping styles you need to look at how much of your response is helpful or self-defeating in terms of taking care of your psyche. For example, as a boss you may feel insecure about what is expected of

you. So in response you may give your subordinates the message that you don't like to hear about problems or bad news. Therefore, you are never faced with potentially threatening and ego-deflating information. However, this strategy, like many ineffective coping strategies, loses its effectiveness over time. If you remain defensive, you might switch to a scapegoating by blaming other people, rather than dealing with the demand or task itself.

3. Am I getting what I want, what I need, and what I intend from this coping strategy? Many ineffective responses continue despite evidence that they do not get us what we want or expect. Look also at the unintentional consequences of your coping behavior. For example, taking a drink when we feel pressure or smoking produces clear long-term negative effects. We may be using up resources to get something managed today that tomorrow will destroy us.

While we have so far explored specific aspects of coping with stressful events, in general we can look at the dysfunctional methods of coping as attempts to manage situations by either exerting too much or too little control over the environment.

Stress Personalities.   Each of us has a predominant style of coping with stressful situations, our "stress personality." The different stress personalities are familiar to us. Some people try to exert too much control over their environment, while others don't exert enough. Of course, the uniqueness of each person cannot be exhausted by our description of personal styles. Also, a person need not be representative of only a single style. Most of us have two or maybe three predominant styles, which we use for different settings or types of situations. We have, for example, styles of coping at home and at work.

Look at the descriptions of stress personalities that are common to undercontrol and to overcontrol. Which personality might be applied to you by the people around you? Write down your three most prevalent stress personalities.

Like most aspects of stress management, these personalities are self-defeating or ineffective only when they become extremes, or when a person becomes so inflexible that he or she responds the same way to all kinds of stress. Each of the following stress personalities is useful in some situations.

Overcontrol Personalities

Take Charge Doer: This person takes on every task because he feels that only he can do it right. He takes over everyone's work and doesn't think of sharing or dividing things. Consequently he is continually overloaded and alone.

Competitor: This person sees every task as a competition between herself and other people. She needs to be the best, to outdo others.

Rescuer: This person feels that his mission in life is to help and do things for another person or all other people. He is always thinking of service, and of the other, although often he does not ask the others if they want help.

Impatient: This person has a short fuse that life is continually setting off. Everything is a source of frustration, even the slightest unexpected event. Frustration is constant.

Angry Demander: This person gets things done by angrily demanding help from others, which often results in the other people not doing the task. This type of leader or co-worker is a source of stress to other people, and is usually not effective in getting what she wants.

Conflict Avoider: This person is a yes-man who will say or volunteer anything just to make sure that people do not clash. This means he never states his real views and ends up doing things that he doesn't want to do or doesn't think should be done. Frustration is likely, but never shown. Everything is held in, as the person tries to satisfy everyone.

Undercontrol Personalities

Helpless Victim: This person feels that she has no power over the events in her life, and that nobody in the environment is out to support her welfare. None of her actions will make a difference, so why try? This person drips with angry self-pity and is full of reasons why circumstances have made her fail.

Anxious Worrier: This person's life is determined by fear of past, present, and future difficulties. He is afraid of failure, which paralyzes him, causing the worst to happen. His mind is occupied with negatives, fears, and self-criticism.

Avoider: This person turns away from responsibilities, tasks, and difficulties. This works at times, but eventually the lack of engagement in problem solving leads to disaster. This strategy is not to be confused with a strategy that aims at a balance of rest and activity and respects the body's needs.

Creative Dreamer: This person is full of plans, ideas, projects, and an intense feeling of creativity, but is not willing to follow through on them. While the positive, creative thinking may offer some stimulation, as it did with the avoider, the lack of activity eventually catches up.

Effective and Ineffective Coping. To conceptualize strategies for coping with stress, it is useful to imagine two extreme coping styles. On the positive end of the spectrum is the *Active Stress Manager* who does what he or she can to plan, anticipate, and respond directly to the pressures and demands. At the negative extreme is the *Passive Victim* of stress who avoids effective action and makes the pressure and demands of his or her life into insuperable obstacles. Most people lie somewhere in between.

ACTIVE STRESS MANAGER	PASSIVE STRESS VICTIM
Puts energy into areas that can be managed	Leaves many things to chance and fate
Anticipates and plans for the future	Does not think ahead
Reservoir of time and energy for the unexpected, unplanned, and crisis events	Faces deadlines by cramming at last minute
	Little foresight or anticipation
Accurate perception of both threats and support from the environment	Takes on tasks that cannot be completed or are overwhelming
	Does not set clear priorities
Takes time to evaluate alternate strategies	Lets problems accumulate
	Sees environment as threatening
Adapts a strategy to reduce stress directly	Compulsive, stereotyped responses to all threatening, stressful situations
Takes care of self and body	Increases level of stress with his or her reaction
Avoids overloading capacity by pacing and relaxing	Lack of pacing, self-care, or diversion
Seeks help and support as much as possible	Works alone, does not call on resources
Manages time by focusing on priorities	

Common Coping Strategies. A recent study of executives by Ari Kiev explored the most common strategies they used in coping with work stress. The researchers also explored the most common strategies used by the healthiest executives.

MOST COMMONLY USED	MOST EFFECTIVE
Change to engrossing nonwork activity	Build resistance with a healthy life-style
Talk over problem with co-workers	Separate and compartmentalize home and work life
Analyze and change strategy for dealing with problem	Regular exercise
Separate and compartmentalize home and work life	Talk over problem with co-workers
Regular exercise	Withdraw from the situation
Talk over problem with spouse	Change to engrossing nonwork activity
Build resistance with a healthy life-style	Talk over problem with spouse
Withdraw from the situation	Work harder on task
Work harder on task	Analyze and change strategy for dealing with problem
Change to different work task	Change to different work task

The most common strategies for coping center on diversion or changing one's way of doing a task. However, the most effective methods, used by healthier people, have to do with taking care of oneself and with moving away from stressful situations (diversion and avoidance). Clearly, self-care and diversion are effective ways to avoid the negative effects of stress and to promote health.

Modifying Your Coping Strategy. Now it is time to do some additional work with your Personal Stress Log. With your awareness of your coping style assets and liabilities, and with the information we have given you about active coping with stress, you can consider and plan new ways to respond to stressful situations.

Read over the list of your most stressful situations. Beginning with the most difficult or pressing, ask yourself these questions:

How much control might I have over this situation? This is a multifaceted question. At first you will be tempted to say that you don't have much control. Yet in our experience everyone underestimates their possible control. For example, you might look at a problem and decide that you can have no effect on it. However, you might gain control when you see that it isn't your problem, and that nobody really expects you to solve it. The sense of freedom comes from increasing control by making the decision that you don't have to handle it. If you come up with other potential ways that you could manage the situation, you will have started to brainstorm about how you might handle it differently.

What are the obstacles to handling this effectively? They might be a lack of time or resources, or a problem with another person who is also involved in the job. Careful analysis and exploration of the nature of the obstacles to responding to a problem is often illuminating. Then think of some of the ways these obstacles might be diminished or neutralized.

How do my personal or emotional responses or sensitivities get in my way? Here you will look at how habits of managing situations, emotional hurts, and prior expectations interfere with change in your ways of responding.

What are alternate ways to manage this situation? This is the time to draw up a list of all the other ways that you might think about and react to this situation. You might find it hard to think of yourself doing things differently, so maybe you can think instead of how other people you know would handle it. The point is to let yourself brainstorm about alternatives, not to evaluate them or plan anything new.

Remember the guidelines for change at the end of Chapter 1. Don't expect to draw up a plan and just make changes in your response. Rather all you need to do first is to develop a mind-set that accepts your willingness and commitment to making changes.

The easiest way to start is with imagination. This is a method that peak performers such as athletes use. Sit in a quiet place, close your eyes, and in your imagination go over every step of the reaction to pressure that is ineffective or that you want to change. Try to imagine every detail of the event or difficulty as it occurred in the past. Pay attention also to any physical and emotional reactions that you can recall, and the reactions of those around you.

Now let yourself imagine the event taking place again, but this time imagine yourself reacting differently. Make it clear to yourself that you do not have to react differently in action, you are merely playing with other ways to react. Try to imagine yourself doing something different as clearly and vividly as your last recall. You will not find it hard to envision how your body will react to the new behavior, and what other consequences will result. In effect you are trying out new possibilities in the laboratory of your imagination.

Do this exercise again, this time imagining a second alternate way of managing the situation. You will begin to see that you have an almost infinite variety of responses.

Now let yourself reflect on the difficulties and unintended consequences of your way of managing this type of situation. Then select a new way of responding that seems feasible and achievable by you. Imagine yourself doing this. Reflect on your fears and feelings about actually changing in practice. If you feel ready to try something different, make a commitment to yourself to do what you imagine the next time a similar stress arises.

Risk, Change, and Growth.   At the start of this chapter the research by Kobasa on stress-resistant personalities was mentioned. One of the three qualities of such personalities was an openness to novelty and change. Some people are naturally open to experiment, while others are more conservative and rigid. However, one cannot be effective at managing the kinds of pressure that most of us face in our lives without understanding that all of life involves change. Every moment we are changing, inside and outside. Thus the possibility of stability or doing things the same way over and over is not open to us. If demands and pressures change, and if we change as well as we grow and gain experience, we need to modify our responses to our world.

We need to feel a sense of being in control of the things that matter to us, and that sense has been linked to active, direct management of situations. In order to accomplish this we need to learn flexibility in our responses.

As you begin to make changes in your responses to pressure, you will encounter various types of emotional resistance. You may feel or say things like, "I just can't" or "That just isn't me." Or you may experience fear about doing things differently, especially if it means facing situations you have avoided in the past. *All* change efforts encounter fear and resistance. That is why psychologists say that making changes involves risk. Risk is not simply danger from outside, but the danger of hurt to our psyche as well. Ironically, in order to overcome pressure we have to risk the very hurt that our psyche wants to avoid. We need to ask people to do things, and submit our work to others for their evaluation. We may experience rejection, confrontation, conflict, and disconfirmation. However, if we do not take the risk, we foreclose the possibility of experiencing success, confirmation, affirmation, and increased self-esteem. More often than not our fears are unrealistic and inaccurate. Things seldom are as bad or as frightening as we imagine them to be.

Achieving greater personal power and coping with pressure involve taking psychological risks. All the exercises and changes the authors suggest in later chapters ask you to move toward doing things that involve psychological risk. Yet, if there is no risk, there is very little chance of growth. Many of the strategies that you will attempt will involve taking personal risks—saying new things, trying new things, and entering new situations. But a person can grow and expand only to the degree that he or she moves into new territory.

The ultimate stability is death. If a person is to stay alive and resist illness and difficulty, he or she must grow, change, expand, and take in new circumstances. Demands and pressures are a part of life, and we need to think about our ways of responding to them. Stress symptoms and burnout are both signs that we are going against our natural human grain and struggling to keep things from changing when the environment and ourselves both resist.

Time Management: Making the Most Out of What You Have

For many people stress takes the concrete form of the clock. Time is the enemy—because there isn't enough of it to get things done. Clearly, however, it is not time but the way that a person relates to it that creates stress. Many people have written about time management since the pioneering book by Alan Lakein, *How to Get Control of Your Time and Your Life*. Time management is not being intimidated by time, but looking at how you approach and organize tasks to make sure that you accomplish what you want, instead of finding yourself doing what you don't want or need to do.

Everyone has at one time or another pleaded with the powers that be for just a little more time. Since neither scientific nor even psychic powers have yet developed a way to increase the length of an hour or a day, learning to manage the time that you do have is the next best thing. In essence time management is a combination of how you think about using the time you have and how you actually use your time. This section discusses approaches to more effective time management and gives you specific techniques that have proved useful to others.

There are two major ways of modifying how you use your time—from the inside and from the outside. How you think about a task has a lot to do with how you approach it. Do you think of how overwhelming this vast project is, or do you break it down into manageable steps and then proceed? The latter is an example of managing from the inside. On the other hand, distractions and pressures from the outside may be the major determinant in your ability to complete a project. If you have too many phone calls or visitors, you can't think clearly and will have trouble getting your work done on schedule.

Working in Chaos—Modifying the Mess. We've all been in a situation where our environment is just too distracting to get anything done. Noise from the outside, interruptions, clutter, a general feeling of disorder. Environmental distractions often play a big part in eating up our precious time. Tension is created any time we begin a task that is surrounded by chaos. Juggling too many tasks takes up thinking space that could be used for other work. Making a list of things to be done releases you from the chaos and focuses your attention on the task at hand.

Take a look at your work area. Is it a paper forest, overrun with underbrush and fallen pine needles? Then it's time to create a parking place for all those papers. Organize your papers into bunches by project or category. Make temporary folders where they can rest until you need them, out of sight. Designate one place for papers that you don't know what to do with or that don't seem to be important enough for a file. At the end of the month go through these papers and throw out anything that you haven't needed in the month. Chances are that you won't need it later and if you do, you can probably get a copy from someone else who has not been such a savvy paper prioritizer. In your sorting process keep a folder of papers that can be read in odd moments, when you are on hold on the phone or in between meetings. This quick-stop file can be useful for things that are not of immediate importance but that do need to come to your attention.

Now that you have created parking places for all your papers make it a goal that you will handle a paper only once. Pick it up and make a decision about what to do with it. Shuffling papers over and over again leads only to not getting anything done. A well-known time management expert tells how he broke himself of paper shuffling. Whenever he picked up a paper he would tear a one-inch strip off the bottom. As his papers became shorter and shorter he began to understand how much time he was spending passing his papers around. Another modification of this is to put a red dot on the paper each time you handle it. The freckled look will begin to give you an idea of how much time you waste.

The Timing of Interruptions.   All of us need some continuous thinking time. A recent study of time usage showed that on the average people are interrupted every ten minutes! Gaining this important thinking time is often the result of creatively managing the external environment to reduce outside stimulation. Some companies have created strategic companywide "quiet time" at a certain hour of the day when everyone agrees not to call or otherwise interrupt anyone else. Some have created a flag system for their doors: a red flag means do not disturb, a green flag means it's okay to come in. It's important that there be places where people can get away to have quiet time. Conference rooms and special "think tanks" can be created to allow people to organize their work. One executive found herself in such a chaotic situation within the office that she often went to her car in the parking lot to gain some uninterrupted silence.

Your situation may not be as desperate as hers, but there are certainly times when people dash into your office wanting attention right now. Closing the door minimizes this, but it also gives people the feeling of your unavailability. A useful strategy might be to meet people at their desks. It's often a compliment to them and it enables you to get up and "let them get back to their work" in a friendly manner.

Another powerful interruption is the telephone. Most businesspeople allow the phone to interrupt them at will. Many people have even found that they have a psychological dependency on the telephone, needing to respond to it no matter when and where. In this case the phone is mastering you, not vice versa. What can you do to manage your phone time? The first strategy is not to get on the phone in the first place. Have someone else screen your calls or hold them until you can call back. Some people set up call-back times when they return calls. Use closed ended questions, ones that can be answered with a yes or no, to keep conversations to the point.

Meeting the Test. The need to manage longer and larger conversations occurs in everyday meetings. If there is an area of business that fits Parkinson's Law it is meetings. The task seems to expand to the time allowed to it. Meetings are important arenas of decision making, information sharing, and idea generation. What's important is to know why you are having the meeting, what items are to be discussed there, and what decisions are to be made. This information should be made available beforehand in an agenda so people will be prepared and focused when they arrive. Getting meetings to begin on time is crucial. Locking the door to the meeting room makes it clear that lateness will not be tolerated. Schedule a ten-minute meeting for 2:00 and leave at 2:10, no matter how many stragglers are only just arriving. To shorten the meeting time stand up throughout the meeting. This tends to decrease the discussion and move people toward faster decisions. Make sure a meeting is the appropriate way to handle a matter.

Don't use $100 of staff time to make a decision worth $25. Schedule meetings to end at the beginning of lunch or 5:00. You'll be surprised how often your sessions end on time. Constantly ask yourself and those present how you can make this meeting more effective and better next time.

Deciding to Decide. Indecision and procrastination are two of the biggest wastes of time. Stopping to weigh all the factors involved and then come to a decision often leaves you in the dust and makes your carefully crafted decision out of date. Think about your decision-making style in terms of a strikeout average. Babe Ruth was the king of home runs as well as of strikeouts. He wasn't afraid to swing at a ball that looked as if it had potential for a hit. This netted him numerous strikeouts but at the same time produced more winners than anyone else. Sticking your neck out in decision making increases the chances of you being right more often.

If you find yourself being indecisive, write down your areas of question and then list your reasons for and against. This prevents you from going round and round in a circle. If you are still indecisive, look at your expectations of yourself for perfection. How much perfection do you expect from yourself? How much excessive effort do you expend to meet this expectation? How much is this costing you in time and effort? Your internal standards may be making extra work for you and keeping you from work that would have a higher payoff.

Help yourself focus on items that have potential by asking yourself what's in it for you when you finish the project. Check your motivation to complete it. Unless you receive some sort of recognition, monetary reward, or personal feeling of accomplishment, you may find yourself conflicted about finishing the project.

If after asking yourself these questions you still find yourself putting off a project, chances are you feel that the project is too large to take on or impossible to finish. What is often paradoxically true about projects of this nature is that they in fact have the highest payoff because of their complexity and their long-term, strategic impact on the business. High payoff items are often vague, difficult to do, and do not fit easily into timetables. They need some special approaches to make them manageable.

When undertaking a project that is hard to begin because of its complexity or size, break it into steps or stages. If there aren't any, create them—"by the inch it's a cinch." When working on large projects get a partner who will encourage you toward your goals. He or she doesn't have to understand exactly what you are doing, but just share your enthusiasm. Meet regularly to form a support team, call each other when you're discouraged. Acknowledge the complexity of what you have undertaken and keep your goal in sight. Decide on a payoff when you finish the project and reward yourself with it.

When working on a number of different projects at the same time it's helpful to keep Pareto's principle in mind: 20 percent of what you do nets 80 percent of your results. The most effective use of time is when it is used on projects that will produce the most results. Focus on the results rather than the process. Target the projects that will make the most difference in the long-range objectives of your company or department. Many people confuse effectiveness with efficiency. Efficiency is doing anything right; effectiveness is doing the right thing right. Get the low payoff items out of the way as quickly as possible so that you can focus all your attention on the high payoff items. Don't get caught stomping ants while there are iguanas climbing the walls.

Part II

SHARING AND CONNECTING

CHAPTER 4

Creating Support Systems and Networking

SKILLS FOR BUILDING SUPPORT AND CONNECTING

We live within a web, a network of relationships with others—family, co-workers, friends, service professionals, and acquaintances. Indeed we cannot think of ourselves as separate from our relationships. Our sense of who we are, our self-worth, comes out of the care and responses from the people closest to us. What we are capable of doing is similarly dependent on whom we have around us and whom we know to call upon. The essential goods and services of human life, both tangible and intangible, derive from the people around us. When we are under pressure, when we experience stress, we rarely handle it entirely on our own. We draw on the experiences and encouragement of friends, and we seek solace and caring from our loved ones. If we lack any of these supportive resources, our test will be that much more difficult, that much more demanding.

Coping with stress and avoiding burnout, then, depend not only on our inner resources and abilities, but on the quality, quantity, and range of the community of people who inhabit our lives. We live within various social networks, such as the personal relationships from which we receive emotional support, maintain a positive personal identity, and obtain resources, information, services, and access to more social contacts. Each of us has several types of networks, and in a sense who we are is defined by who we connect to. These networks act as social support groups. The process of activating the web of contacts and people you know to help you get something accomplished, or for help, is what we will call "networking." In overcoming stress and burnout the abilities to create supportive relationships and to network are essential. In addition, studies of personal health and effective work performance and success all cite the existence of strong support systems and personal networks as of critical importance.

Burnout and health are not individual qualities. They arise out of our environment, the essence of which is our relationships to people. Our health is determined by the nature of our involvement with others, and the helpfulness and personal support that we receive. "Friends can be good medicine" is the slogan of the campaign of the California Department of Mental Health. This chapter explores how you can develop support systems and become an effective networker so that other people can help you manage stress and accomplish your goals.

First, we look at your own networks and social support system, assessing the degree and quality of your connection to other people. The principles of networking and resource sharing are then outlined.

Think about all the people in your life who in one way or another give you encouragement. This could be verbal support, nonverbal looks, or even just that those people are on your side. A support system is a resource pool, on which you can draw selectively to support you to move in the direction of your choice. Through this encouragement you end up feeling stronger about yourself. The people around you, especially those closest to you, help to validate your competence and self-worth; they can pitch in when you need to get things done, offer information and resources, help you cope with difficulties, provide a willing ear for emotional support and caring, and help you gain new competencies, undertake new challenges, and attain objectives.

When you go out on a sunny day, the glare of sunlight on your unprotected eyes creates stress and makes it difficult to see. Many people use sunglasses to filter out the harmful rays. We can think of stressors and stressful life situations in a similar way. If we have to handle them alone, they will be difficult and we may be overwhelmed. But when we have help from other people, we can accomplish tasks and respond to pressure much more easily, with less pain and damage.

Think about a difficult task or demand—moving to another house, taking a new job in a new city, beginning a major new work project. You might become overwhelmed by doing all this alone or even with the help of a supportive friend or spouse. Imagine how it would be if other people in your family and some friends pitch in to help with all the tasks. Imagine that people from the new job meet you and invite you to their house, and help you find your way around the new city.

The Nature of Support

By "social support" we mean a series of relationships with significant people with whom we share common experiences. What makes them different from acquaintances is a sense of connectedness that comes from a shared experience or belief system. These people form a net and provide a "social inoculation" from everyday pressures and crises. In addition, they provide valuable problem-solving information, remind us of who we are, aside from this particular stressful situation, and give us a sense of belonging where we are valued for ourselves.

It is hard for many people to maintain these long-lasting relationships because of geographic mobility. We often experience disruption in the relationships we have formed and find it difficult to maintain those connections over time. This mobility is embedded in the very values our society holds dear. We emphasize the importance of individual effort and initiative, which has led us to a life-style where we have a strong sense of competition and individual responsibility, often keeping us from seeking support of any kind.

Instead, using a concept that Alvin Toffler popularized in *Future Shock*, we need to learn to create and sustain less permanent, temporary relationships. If we move to a new job every few years, we quickly need to discover the people in the company who know how to get things done, and make contact not only with our direct work group but also with a broader group of employees so that we can have a sense of the company as a whole and feel at home within it. Similarly, facing the frequency of divorce and temporary intimate relationships, we have to learn to make relationships with people who can care for us, even if that care and support does not last forever. Finding support, creating relationships, and making connections are skills that we need to develop to operate in a world of change. Even though your personal support networks will be in flux, you need to be aware of that, and develop and nurture the relationships that you do have.

People Need People: Loners Get Sick

The quality and quantity of help that we receive have been found to be the major determining factor in how well we cope with stressful situations. Research studies show that the greater our social networks and the number of people available to help us, the healthier we are likely to be. Both physical and mental health are connected to the presence of helpful and supportive people in one's family, community, and work environment.

Recent research has proved that human connectedness helps you live longer. Married people, especially husbands, live longer than single people. People have a greater likelihood of getting sick or dying during the year or so after the loss of a loved one, or the loss of something central in their life. A large-scale study found that the people with more social ties had lower death rates regardless of their sex, race, social class, smoking, alcohol consumption, physical activity, obesity, eating patterns, or use of health services. Even people who have pets have a better survival rate after a heart attack than non-pet owners. Another set of studies shows that healthy people can be distinguished by the number of people in their networks and the amount of two-way exchange, helping and being helped, within these units. People with emotional problems had fewer social contacts. It's not clear exactly what it is that makes the difference, but one theme runs through these studies—being connected to other people is a powerful protector of overall health and well-being.

Mapping Your Support Networks.   Since social support is an important factor in surviving everyday stress and strain, it's time to examine what your social support networks look like.

You can think of personal support networks as a series of rings around you, which act as cushions to lessen the effect of whatever stress occurs. A large, varied support network, or a small, tight, intimate network are both helpful. The type of support network and the number of people in your life who are available to you, of course, depend on the type of person you are. Some of us are gregarious, while others are more introverted and may have only a few close friends. However, what seems to be important is not the number of people but their relationship to you. The breadth of relationships, providing you with multiple layers of cushioning, seems to be an important factor in maintaining health.

This section contains questions to help you map and explore the several types of social support networks. Exercise 12 is a map with a series of concentric circles. In the innermost circle is the label "me," because you are at the center of each of your social networks. Each succeeding circle represents a different degree of closeness to you. The rings closest to the center are for the people closest to you. The circles are further subdivided into five wedge-shaped sections, each one representing a different context or environment, or a different network: family/relatives, friends, neighbors/community, co-workers, and service/professional resources. There will be of course some overlap; a person may relate to you in more than one category.

Fill in the names of the people in each of your networks, starting with the circle closest to you. You might place a person in several networks, if, for example, she is both a neighbor and a co-worker. Place her corresponding to the degree of closeness you feel for her in that context. For example, you may not see that person much at work, but you may see her every day at home. When you have entered all the names, draw a line between each set of people that know each other. All the people in your family, or in your company, may know each other. Therefore there will be many interconnecting lines. This is your personal network.

EXERCISE 13: NETWORK MAP

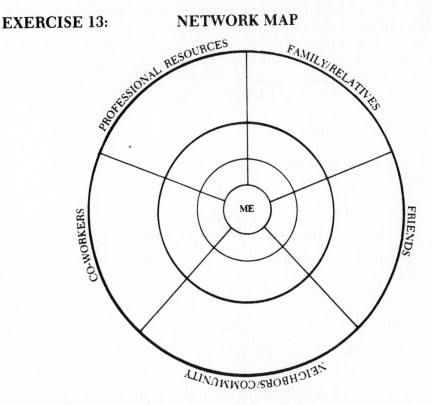

The Major Types of Support Networks

Family or intimate network: Traditionally, there was a nuclear family, spouse and children, and the extended family, living nearby. Today many people are not married, but have developed a family-like network of close friends, lovers, or old roommates who act like a family.

Friendship and community networks: These are the people in your community and your social life, and may even include some people from work with whom you share social time. These are the people you might call on for help in dealing with various stressful situations—moving, breakup of relationship, difficulty on the job, or a personal crisis. These are also the people you see every day, whose children go to the same schools, and on whom you can draw for information and help with household activities and community affairs. They form both your community environment and, in the case of friends, a continuing source of support as you move or change. Often your friends are carriers and historians of your personal history and identity.

Work network: These are the people with whom you work and on whom you could feel free to call for work-related support, advice, or information. These can be mentors, people who take an interest in your career development, or built-in support resources like employee relations staff or employee assistance counselors.

Service and professional network: This network consists of helpers outside your usual pathways, and includes people like clergy, counselors, home repair people, therapists, consultants, and anyone who is a trained helper. One advantage of this network is that you may choose exactly whom you wish to include and make a contractual arrangement with time limits.

Functions of Support Groups. Support networks provide a number of important functions:

>*Role models:* showing you what is possible, what works in certain situations, and alternative approaches

>*Motivation:* reminding you of common interests and goals

>*Nurturance:* friendship and close contact

>*Help:* assistance in times of crisis

>*Mentoring:* respect for your skills and encouragement for new ways to use them

>*Referral:* connection with resources, systems of support, and knowledge of how certain procedures work

>*Challenge:* encouragement to take on new responsibilities, make needed changes, and stretch yourself beyond your present limits

We get different things from different people in our support groups. There are people to play with, work with, teach us, and offer professional advice. Exercise 13 is a list of roles or functions that you might expect from other people. For each function list the one or two most important people to whom you turn. Then go back and estimate on a scale of 1 to 5 how helpful, satisfying, or supportive your contact with that person actually is (1 = not very effective, 5 = very effective).

You may find that you list the same person or set of people several times; many support people perform several functions. As you go through the list you will begin to see patterns. Do you rely on one person too heavily, or are there areas where you cannot think of a support person who is, or might be, available to you? The strengths and weaknesses of your support networks will be clear when you complete this profile.

Family and Personal Support. It comes as no surprise that your family, or the people who are closest to you and live with you, is the most important support group in protecting you from stress. How do

(text continues on page 109)

E X E R C I S E 13

PERSONAL NETWORK PROFILE

The People   How Helpful Are They?
I Turn To: (Scale 1–5)

1. For Close Friendship

_____

2. To Share Problems

_____

3. To Play With

_____

4. For Expert Advice

_____

5. To Energize Me

_____

6. As Teachers

_____

7. As Helpers

_____

8. As Mentors

_____

9. For Acceptance and Approval

_____

10. To Help Me Discover and Try New Things

_____

11. For Professional Contacts and Access

_____

| | The People
I Turn To: | How Helpful Are They?
(Scale 1–5) |

12. For Good Social Time

_____

_____

13. When I Am Hurting

_____

_____

14. When I Need Good Advice with a Problem

_____

_____

15. When I Want to Be with Someone Who Knows Me Well

_____

_____

Look over each of the categories and circle the areas where you feel that you need, or would like, more support. Which members of your network do you rely on too much, and which members might you rely on more often?

SELF-ASSESSMENT: THE STRENGTH OF YOUR SUPPORT NETWORKS

This exercise assesses the quality and level of support in your life in the three major networks: family, friends, and work. After each statement circle the number that best describes how true each statement is for you, as you are feeling now.

I. Family (or Intimate) Support	Very True	Somewhat True	Slightly True	Not True
1. My family (or intimate friends) take time for me when I need it	3	2	1	0
2. My family (or intimate friends) understands when I am upset, and responds to me	3	2	1	0
3. I feel accepted and loved by my family	3	2	1	0
4. My family allows me to do new things and make changes in my life	3	2	1	0
5. My spouse (or partner) accepts my sexuality	3	2	1	0
6. My family gives me as much as I give them	3	2	1	0
7. My family expresses caring and affection to me, and responds to my feelings, such as my anger, sorrow, and love	3	2	1	0
8. The quality of the time I spend with my family is high	3	2	1	0
9. I feel close and in touch with my family	3	2	1	0
10. I am able to give what I would like to my family	3	2	1	0

I. Family (or Intimate) Support (continued)	Very True	Somewhat True	Slightly True	Not True
11. I feel I am important to the people in my family	3	2	1	0
12. I feel that I am honest to the people in my family, and that they are honest to me	3	2	1	0
13. I can ask the people in my family for help when I need it	3	2	1	0
TOTAL I				

A score of 20 or more indicates that you feel a high level of support from your family (or intimate) network.

II. Friendship Support	Very True	Somewhat True	Slightly True	Not True
1. I usually place the needs of others above my own	3	2	1	0
2. I feel I give more than I get from other people	3	2	1	0
3. I find it difficult to share my feelings with other people	3	2	1	0
4. I am not able to give what I would like to other people	3	2	1	0
5. I don't feel cared for or valued by the people around me	3	2	1	0
6. I usually can't find people to spend time with when I want to	3	2	1	0
7. I am often lonely and alone	3	2	1	0
8. I find it hard to ask for what I want	3	2	1	0
9. I don't usually feel close to other people	3	2	1	0

II. Friendship Support (continued)	Very True	Somewhat True	Slightly True	Not True
10. There are few people I can really count on	3	2	1	0
11. Few people know me very well	3	2	1	0
12. People don't seem to want to get to know me	3	2	1	0
13. I tend to hide my sexuality, or feel uncertain about it	3	2	1	0
14. I find it hard to touch other people	3	2	1	0
15. Other people rarely touch or hug me	3	2	1	0
16. I find it hard to ask other people for help	3	2	1	0
17. I am always doing things for other people	3	2	1	0
18. People rarely help me	3	2	1	0
19. When it comes down to it, I feel that I am basically on my own	3	2	1	0
20. I have few friends or people I am close to	3	2	1	0
21. I don't like to spend time with other people	3	2	1	0
22. I feel distant and apart from other people	3	2	1	0
23. I don't expect much from people	3	2	1	0
TOTAL II				

Note that these statements are phrased in negative terms. So in this case, if you have a higher score, you have a less supportive network of friends and acquaintances. A score above 25 indicates that you have weakness in your personal support system and need to take steps to make the relationships you have deeper and more supportive, or to make new and more supportive friendships.

III. Work Support	Very True	Somewhat True	Slightly True	Not True
1. When I run into trouble, there are co-workers I can seek out for help	3	2	1	0
2. The people around me care about me as a person	3	2	1	0
3. I feel I can question and negotiate with supervisors about work assignments	3	2	1	0
4. I am clear about what I am to do and what others expect from me	3	2	1	0
5. I am not usually afraid that co-workers are critical of me behind my back	3	2	1	0
6. People at work are more concerned about getting things done than about competing among themselves	3	2	1	0
7. There are people I talk to each day informally	3	2	1	0
8. I feel my abilities are valued by others at work	3	2	1	0
9. Information is shared freely among people who should know things	3	2	1	0
10. When I can't do something on my own, I can take my problems to others and they will help	3	2	1	0
11. I can ask for guidance and help from superiors	3	2	1	0
12. The climate of my workplace is pleasant and comfortable	3	2	1	0
13. When people are upset about something at work, it is usually talked about	3	2	1	0

III. Work Support (continued)	Very True	Somewhat True	Slightly True	Not True
14. Many things about work are pleasant and enjoyable	3	2	1	0
15. People are given what they need to complete the tasks they are assigned	3	2	1	0
16. There are outlets to help me handle the frustrations and irritations of my work	3	2	1	0
TOTAL III				

Like the family support inventory, this assessment consists of positive statements. A score over 20 indicates a supportive work network and environment.

you feel when you come home? Do you feel loved, safe, happy, protected, and calm? Do you feel angry, frustrated, unsafe, and on guard? Do you feel lonely, unaccepted, neglected, or ignored? The first set of feelings helps your body and psyche relax after the demands and pressures of outside, while the other two response patterns inhibit your attempts to release the stress of the day, or trigger additional defensive stress responses. To manage stress effectively and maintain balance in your life, one of the best resources is a household that is a safe refuge. Even living alone may be preferable to living in an embattled household, in terms of your stress level. Also, having people around you to whom you can turn to share pressures, fears, and struggles is helpful in coping with pressure that cannot be modified. Both friends and family can perform this function.

The support and help from your family, or from the people closest to you in your everyday life, take several forms. There is help with tasks and meeting the day's demands—errands, housework, child care, and financial support. There is also support in having someone to talk to and share things with, for emotional release as well as helpful suggestions and opportunity to reflect on one's life difficulties. There is the knowledge that somebody accepts you as you are and cares for you. And finally, there is the support of having someone to do things with, to share hobbies, leisure activities, and have fun with.

Mobilizing Your Networks

Think again about your personal networks and the support people in your current life. Do you notice some areas in which you would like to increase your resources? Here are some general thoughts about building support.

If people ask themselves why they don't have more friends and support in their work and personal lives, they most often answer that they aren't available. In fact the major obstacles to building more supportive relationships lie in ourselves, not in the environment. We assume incorrectly that the people around us will not like us, do not have the time, aren't interested in what we are doing, or don't want to be helpful. Because of this assumption we don't ask other people things or initiate contact with them. We create a self-fulfilling prophecy. We never find out that our assumptions about other people aren't true, because we never check them out.

The best rule for extending support networks is to seek out other people. Sometimes they won't want to help or do things, but that is not the only response we will receive. Sometimes other people seem to enjoy contact and exchange with you, and even enjoy taking the time to help you. Also, they will then begin to seek your help, which will balance out the relationship. When people begin to reach out to others, almost invariably they find that people are friendly, easy to approach, and helpful.

Another way to extend support is to extend the amount and degree of your social contacts. If you are in the habit of eating lunch or dinner alone, begin to invite others to join you. Get to know people in other areas of your workplace. Studies of successful workers, and workers who cope well with stress, show that they usually cultivate a large number of other people in the organization. Then when a position becomes open, or information about a delicate subject is needed, that person can tap into his or her social network.

It's not what you know but who you know. You can start by knowing other people in your field, utilizing professional organizations and meetings for professional networking. Ask people where they work and what they do. Strike up conversations with co-workers about their civic or social interests. Imagine yourself as a host to the world instead of a guest. Introduce people to each other. Make connections anywhere; talk to people in the line at the supermarket or on the bus. Relationship counts whether it is long-lasting or fleeting. Actively approaching others will set you in the direction of achieving your goals.

Support and Exchange. Social support is not static or fixed. It grows, and can be strained or strengthened, according to the care that you give your networks. When you do not receive the support you need, there can be many reasons. It is possible that you have a lot of support available to you but you are not willing to receive it, or you may not have much support in your ongoing relationships but know where to reach out for it. Look at social support as an exchange of energy from one person to another. People do not exist independently of one another; they participate in many varieties of relationships. Difficulties occur in the area of social support when an imbalance in this energy exchange occurs. Since most people do not keep elaborate track of each exchange of support, it is possible to get out of balance when you have given too much and not taken back enough support to keep going. Even cars have to stop for tune-ups.

The authors have talked about social support as the caring and giving that goes on between people, exchanging both emotional and physical help. But we haven't talked about the two other areas of exchange that help to rebalance your life: self-support, things you do for yourself; and receiving the care that others give to you. People often feel more comfortable with one method of exchange and concentrate their activities in that direction. Research and common sense suggest that we manage stress best when we participate actively in all three types of exchange. The other two areas of exchange are discussed in greater depth in Chapter 6 and are mentioned here as reminders that social support is just one part of a complex of exchange and renewal mechanisms.

Building Support by Personal Networking.   Networking is the process of expanding, nurturing, and mobilizing the people you know. Network building is a general process that we do all the time; every meeting and phone call maintains our personal networks. In times of transition or crisis or extreme pressure and stress, the best coping strategy is often mobilizing a personal network. For example, say you are job hunting. One way to do it is to call the network of people you know who are in your field or who might know people in your area, who in turn might be aware of a job. A few phone calls mobilize your network by making people aware that you have a need. You will also gather useful information and a further set of contacts. Thus your friend might say that she has an ex-roommate who works at a certain company that she heard was looking for a marketing person. Another phone call, and the chain, which grows out of your personal network, grows. Career development consultants say that for each person, the right job lies about three links along this chain.

Networks and chains of connections are the primary way that things get done in society, and the way that information is transferred. Unlike formal organizational structures, networks are formless, extensive, amorphous, and infinitely flexible. Think about your own organization. You will probably notice that the people who are most effective at their work are often those with large informal networks within the organization. They know how to get things done and to find things out. They have friends in every division and they do favors for others. In turn they can count on others for help. Networks thrive on balance. The degree to which others see you as helpful, as a good resource, and as supportive determines how they will respond to your needs. Generally, the most effective networks are those which flow in both directions.

Let us say that you have a problem, which is a source of pressure or stress in your life. Personal networking is a helpful way to move toward solution. Write down a pressing problem on a piece of paper. Next list all the people whom you know, even slightly, who might be a resource for this problem. That includes people who might have relevant information, people who have been through similar situations or crises, or people who might relate to or have something to do with your problem. Then think about how each of them might be helpful. Begin to contact them, discuss your difficulty or need with them, and ask if they can help. Be sure to let them know what you need, or what sort of help they might be able to offer. Few people are willing to enter into vague or open-ended commitments.

The major part of networking is the process of making a chain to link yourself to resources. Each person in your network has his or her own network. By tapping into your own network, you can tap into the networks of each person you know. The potential reach of your personal network is limited only by your imagination.

The willingness to network and seek resources and help is an important aspect of dealing with problems and stress. Good networkers are able to find more ways to cope with their problems than people who keep their difficulties to themselves and do not tap the expertise.

Differences between Men and Women. Just as each individual's support network is composed of different people in the various groupings, there are also differences in the way men and women compose their networks. On the whole it seems that women know more about developing their support networks and making use of them. In *Intimate Strangers*, Lillian Rubin provides numerous examples of this pattern. Rubin found that women share their deepest secrets but men rarely confide in each other. Men list fewer relationships than women and their friendships have a different content and quality than those described by women, more talk about feelings and personal experience by women versus more information giving and opinion sharing by men. Male relationships are based more on a shared activity, like a sport or job, whereas women's relationships tend to focus on more sensitive life events. Two-thirds of the single men Rubin interviewed were unable to name a best friend, and when they did have a friend it was likely to be a woman. There are some differences with married couples. Married women tend to resume their intimate friendships with women after marriage while men tend to develop an intimate relationship with their spouse. This may explain some of the research findings that report the benefits of being married for men—they are able to create more intimate relationships within the framework of marriage.

Men, on the other hand, benefit from a different sort of network. From their school days in team sports through various clubs and organizations and fraternities men seem to form fraternal and friendship groups. These groups perform many functions, in addition to socializing and blowing off steam. The "old boy network" forms a resource pool of potential recruits for jobs, information, services, and other activities. This is useful and helpful for those who are "in," but penalizes those who are not part of these informal, often long-standing, networks. Thus women, as they enter the executive market, have begun to form their own "old girl networks" to offer themselves these same advantages. The extent of these networks is critical to many personal needs. For example, if one needs a lawyer or contractor, or wants to know something about government regulations, or is looking for a new job, this kind of network is the first one that is consulted. Many jobs, bits of information, and opportunities travel almost exclusively along such networks. Not being connected to some of them is a handicap, and can make coping with any pressure or difficulty harder.

Ideas for Generating Support

This chapter has explored ways to mobilize and expand the effectiveness of your personal support networks. As a final note, here are some general guidelines for increasing the effectiveness of your personal support networks:

- Ask for direct help and be receptive when it is offered
- List six people with whom you would like to improve your relationship and list one action step you will be willing to take toward this improvement
- Rid yourself of relationships that are not supportive or are damaging to you
- Maintain high-quality relationships on and off the job by telling them how much you value their support
- Review your present network and make an honest assessment of how well it is working for you, and identify areas where you could use some changes
- Keep your energy exchange balanced, return favors and thoughtfulness

Additional suggestions for extending your social support networks are offered in other parts of this book. The following chapters on communication and basic assumptions about yourself offer more thoughts on how you keep yourself from reaching out and using the help that is available to you.

CHAPTER 5

Skills for Working Together

Few of us can hope to manage the stresses of our lives alone. The extent to which we enter into working, helping relationships with the people around us is a potent indicator of how well we deal with stress. Going it alone is rarely an effective way to get things done.

We often think of getting along and working well with other people as a personality trait: some of us have it, some of us don't. Certainly, some people do it better than others. However, we can also think of working well with others as interpersonal skills that can be learned. While many aspects of getting along with people seem to come naturally to some people, there are few, if any, people who simply can't learn to get along with others. We have found that people who are pure loners, if they are to remain healthy and manage stress, must arrange a very special working and personal life to meet their needs.

CREATING WORK GROUP SKILLS

Few tasks can be accomplished in isolation; people are always joining together to get things done. This creates a host of questions. Who will be in charge and make decisions? How will work be distributed and tasks divided up? Who will be responsible for the quality? Who will receive the credit? While groups often have a person who is officially in charge, in fact group power is usually distributed. People have power when they control resources, or particular skills, or have access to information that the leader may not.

Important skills in working well with people involve creating harmony and unity of purpose, and balancing your personal needs with those of the group.

The major skills of creating effective work groups have to do with active listening, assertion, resolving conflicts, and mobilizing human resources effectively. All of these skills require that you pay attention to yourself and others. When a group or task is being organized, people who want things to go well and minimize stress pay attention to the process happening between them, the way they are going about things. They ask questions of each other, such as how should we do this, who has the skills, and are there feelings that anyone needs to air. Each member of the group attempts to be aware of others' feelings, and also his or her own.

Chapter 4 looked at bringing people into your life. The challenge discussed in this chapter is how to keep them there in productive ways. Social support isn't much good if the relationships with your supporters don't work. You may have people in your network who don't provide you with as much support as they could because you have an unresolved conflict, or you have a problem communicating your needs. You may have some long-lasting disagreement related to your interests or feelings that keeps you from being as helpful as you could.

The skills of working with people are needed in one's family, in the community, and at work. The strength of your personal support is not something that you are blessed with, but is a result of your application of the skills. Some people exhibit these skills instinctively, while others have to work to learn them.

Reflect on your ways of working with people. Where are your strengths? What areas give you the most difficulty? Do you feel that deficiencies in working with others has been a major liability to you, adding to your life stress? Are people usually a problem and source of stress to you, or are they a source of help and support?

Certain skills help people work together. At the core are the skills of communicating—saying clearly what you want and mean, and being open to the messages of others. While most of us feel we do this instinctively, in fact, blockages in communication can and often do cripple work groups.

A constant of personal relationships is conflict. Some people do not get along, and at other times, conflicts—real or imagined—erupt between co-workers. These can paralyze a group. A conflict that smolders below the surface can create stress for everyone. Some people are so difficult and create so much negativity that they can be labeled "stress carriers." Dealing with them productively is an important stress reduction skill.

This chapter reviews some cornerstones of communications skills, active listening, assertion skills, and conflict resolution.

ACTIVE LISTENING

Listening to other people involves more than just hearing their words. It includes hearing the undertones and emotional shadings, which may amplify or seemingly conflict with what they say. Tone of voice and nonverbal behavior tell us how the other person feels about us, about what he is saying, and about himself. Sometimes we need to ask about these emotional undertones. For example, we might ask if something is making him angry, rather than assume he is angry at us or try to guess whether he is angry at something. The question can relieve our own uncertainty and make the conversation easier when the feeling is out in the open. We need to be aware of emotional undertones as well as the content of messages.

Taking the time to clarify and understand what other people are saying is a way to build, solidify, and mobilize help and support for any task. When we feel that another person is *really* listening to us, we feel more positively toward her. Listening clearly helps people feel good about each other. It also helps them work together to solve problems. Most important, it cuts down on the needless stress caused by not understanding, by having to guess or worry about what the other person really meant or really had to say.

All of us need to learn to listen more effectively. One way to increase your listening acuity is to break listening down into three steps: making contact, clarifying, and negotiation among options.

Making contact: this is when you begin the conversation. Your immediate goal is to put the other person at ease. Pay attention to his nonverbal cues—is he moving back because you are standing too close? how is he holding his arms? how often does he look you in the eye? In addition, it is important to turn some of your attention toward yourself and notice how you are feeling. What are you experiencing—excitement, apprehension, fear, enthusiasm? What does that emotion feel like in your body and how is it manifested? How easy is it for you to be in contact with this person? Noticing your discomfort is an opportunity to reassess your response and change it if you want. You are not stuck with one approach to a situation; you can change your experience by changing your mind about how you want to perceive the situation. For example, think of someone you work with or come into contact with regularly. Picture her as your enemy, someone for whom you have strong dislike. Notice how your body reacts to these thoughts. Now think of the person again, as if she were one of your closest friends and supporters, and notice what happens in your body this time. You can change how your body feels by changing your thoughts. Try this on other situations where you have a strong opinion about someone: switch it to the opposite feeling in your imagination and see what happens the next time you come in contact with him or her.

Clarification: the second step in active listening begins when you acknowledge the situation. Is there a problem that needs to be solved, a conflict, a confusion, a shared interest? Define the situation and the feelings of that situation. Tell the other person what impact the situation is having on you and what you would like to see happen. Tell him what you've heard and understood him to have said to you and what you understand of his assessment of the situation. Notice what he felt, intended, and observed. This is an important step because it sets the groundwork for the problem solving. Make sure you spend enough time at this stage so that both of you feel heard and understood.

Negotiation among options: this is the time to explore what can be done about the situation now that both of you have been able to say what you want and what you think is happening. Now is the time to have a dialogue about your views and ideas, using your listening and clarifying skills. Be prepared to negotiate; there is often a solution between the two views you and your partner hold. Seek solutions. This will not necessarily result in a resolution in one discussion. You may have to take a break and come back to the process several times after each of you has had some time to think. What you have done is to initiate a process whereby you will have a vehicle to know what the other person is thinking and feeling in an atmosphere where you do not become adversaries but helpmates in a negotiation process.

This process will take more time than your previous perfunctory discussions. But before long you will begin to reap the benefits of these additional clarification and negotiation steps in the form of an expanded work and personal support base.

Assertion Skills

In order to engage in this negotiation process it is helpful to be able to speak easily about what you want. Many people experience difficulties in expressing their needs and desires and find that assertion skills enhance their ability to get what they want in personal and professional situations. A brief review of assertion skills will give you a model for approaching others.

Many people are afraid to ask others for what they want, or assume they don't even have the right to ask for things. They ignore their needs for help and information and either try to get what they want indirectly, or get it for themselves. Other people are able to ask, but they do so with aggression or antagonism that destroys the goodwill of the other person. There are many reasons for this. You might be afraid of rejection, or someone saying "no," or you might doubt the goodwill of other people to the extent that you feel you have to intimidate them.

When we work with other people we need many things. We are continually in the position of having to ask others for help and for information. If doing that is stressful, and if our fears lead us to avoid asking, then we cut ourselves off from potential resources and support. It is essential that we be aware of what we want or need from other people, and be able to ask for it without demanding it. Being assertive means standing up for your own rights without violating the rights of others. It does not necessarily mean being hostile or aggressive.

In order to increase your assertiveness you need to identify the difference among the three styles of possible responses in any situation.

Aggressive style: implies an attack on the other person, and is loaded with past annoyance. The intention of the communication is usually to hurt the other person and the result is to build up more resentment.

Passive style: results in one person giving in when he or she really doesn't want to, and usually manifests itself later in some more disguised form of retaliation.

Assertive style: focuses on solving some problem in a way where both people are winners. Requests in this approach ask for some specific action and indicate a willingness to negotiate to a mutually agreeable solution.

Now identify an area or type of situation in your job or personal relationships in which you want to experiment with being more assertive. Choose an area where you do not get what you want. In choosing the behavior that you want to change, make sure that it is mildly to moderately uncomfortable, not highly upsetting. In beginning any behavior change experiment it's important not to build in failure at the start. You might want to make some notes to remind you who is involved, when does this situation happen, what bothers you about it, how you deal with it now, what fears you have about the situation, and what outcome you want. Once the situation is clearly in mind, it's time to set up a plan of action.

Think back to your goal and make sure it is clear and simple. If you don't know where you are going, you won't end up where you want to go. Know what the problem is, see it from both your side and the other person's side. Arrange a time to discuss the situation when you can both have time to consider options. When you meet describe how you feel with "I" messages, owning your experience and not blaming it on the other person. For example, "I have been feeling like you haven't been listening to my suggestions in staff meeting for the last three weeks and I would like you to give my ideas consideration. I feel like participating more and being part of the office team."

It might be helpful to you to write out your assertive script ahead of time and practice in front of a mirror or with a friend to get some direct feedback on your approach. Pay attention to the body messages you are giving. Assertive body language is an important part of communicating the intent of your message. To communicate your intention clearly:

- maintain direct eye contact
- stand or sit up straight
- speak clearly with a firm tone
- emphasize your points with gestures
- visualize your ideal outcome while you are speaking

The last step toward becoming assertive is to learn how to counter some of the responses you may receive when you assert yourself. Often people won't want to respond to what you have so clearly told them. They will laugh off your assertion, try to change the subject, shift the conversation in another direction, or even respond by attacking you. In each of these and many other variations you will need to reassert your intention to clarify a situation so that your rights are taken into consideration. You may do this by calmly repeating your point and not getting sidetracked. You may shift the conversation from the topic (content) to how the person is feeling (process) and then back to the topic again. Or you may have to prompt the other person to tell you exactly what is bothering him or her in order to get a better idea of how to frame your assertion. These and other approaches will be necessary to maintain your intent of communicating your point of view in potentially difficult situations.

CONFLICT MANAGEMENT

Conflict is the result of any kind of opposition or antagonistic interaction between two or more parties. Conflict cannot exist if one of the parties does not perceive that it exists. Conflicts are normal and natural consequences of human interaction and they occur for multiple reasons: internal stress coming from one person, which overflows into the workplace; incompatible expectations among workers and work groups; differences over how to get a job done, values, orientations, and desired outcomes; increasing complexity within the organization resulting in more ambiguous work roles; and external pressures and crises from the environment. In this century there have been three stages in thinking about conflict. Up until the mid-1940s conflict was seen as destructive and people believed it should be eliminated by management. This view changed in the early 1950s when people began to recognize that conflict was inevitable in organizations and was a necessary evil to be "resolved." This perspective is still predominant in business settings today. Recently there has been yet another way to think about organizational conflict—as a positive force for change. If an organization deliberately chooses to "manage" or "resolve" conflict, it is depriving itself of needed change and adaptation capability that enhances its capacity to survive. Opposition and conflict can in some cases stimulate thinking in new directions. Changes do not just happen; they are often inspired by conflict. Without conflict an organization cannot survive. Functional levels of conflict have been shown to be related to innovation and higher-quality decisions.

It is important to differentiate between functional and dysfunctional conflict. The demarcation between these two types of conflict is neither clear nor precise. One factor may be how well the conflict functions to create a healthy and positive involvement toward one's group goals and the larger organization's goals. If the conflict is perceived as stimulating and creating challenge, more often than not it will lead to improved organizational and individual performance. If the conflict is perceived as divisive and alienating, then it will tend to produce less productive responses. Some management theorists argue that a company can have too little conflict for its own good and may need to adapt techniques and strategies to increase productive conflict. One way to think about conflict in this new format is on a conditional basis, carefully analyzing the situation and assessing the advantages and disadvantages of conflict in each particular case.

Sources of conflict fall into three general categories: communication, structure, and personal behavior. Conflicts in communication arise from misunderstandings and other difficulties in the general communication network. Structural conflict occurs from roles and barriers that are built into the organizational system. Personal factors include individual values and behaviors that conflict with others'. In each case it is important first to assess the source of the conflict and then choose the best approach to ameliorate the problem. There are as many approaches as there are kinds of conflict and the authors will not give you a cookbook of recipes for each kind. Instead we provide a way of thinking about conflict in a positive manner, as a source of problem solving and an opportunity for creativity.

Dealing with difficult people.

One common area of conflict is that in any organization there are difficult people to work with. These people can be thought of as stress carriers. They are often disruptive, they bully and overpower others, they complain about everything and have a generally negative attitude. They may express this attitude openly or make their views known silently. These people make it difficult to keep up everyday productivity and may be especially difficult in situations that require innovative problem solving. We all know what a source of stress it can be to work with such people. Curiously, they create stress in others but often feel little stress within themselves. They project their tensions onto the people around them, creating toxic environments.

Not all "difficult people" are always that way. They may be tired, frightened, or just having a bad day. They may be difficult only in interaction with a single person—you. But in general a difficult person is one whose undesirable behavior is repetitive and widespread. The difficult behavior is not a onetime occurrence, nor is it usually confined to one person.

To work with a difficult person one must analyze the interactions. Understand who is playing what role, and why. Borrowing from the psychologist Eric Berne, we can see each person as having three interchangeable states—superior, peer, and subordinate. Each has its own set of behaviors, and one may exhibit all three at any one time.

What often happens in an interaction with a difficult person is that he or she responds inappropriately. To see how this might look in everyday interaction, view yourself as a series of three circles, one for each state, and the other person another series of circles. When you are interacting successfully, you are communicating from the same state—i.e., peer to peer. Major problems arise when one person communicates from one state and the other person responds from another state, say, superior to peer. In this case difficult behavior is simply a symptom of a transaction gone bad. Dealing with difficult behavior involves re-creating parallel lines of communication through a change in the state of one or both people. Since you are often the one to notice this inequity in the communication, you can most easily adjust the situation. Sometimes it's helpful to tell the other person that you feel he or she is talking to you in an "unequal" way and you think that you could best solve the problem if you were both on the same wavelength. Sometimes just stopping one conversation enables you to start another one on a more mutual basis. However, some people are so accustomed to a particular state, such as the superior mode, that they don't realize that they are using it all the time, inappropriately. It usually takes a more direct approach, which will be described a little later, to help them reorient their behavior.

The authors have talked about a communication framework for identifying miscommunication leading to difficult behavior. In addition to miscommunication there are other styles of difficult behavior, which can be divided into two basic categories: passive and aggressive. The aggressive person needs to be stopped in his tracks so you can deal with him; the passive person needs to be provoked into action. The aggressive person uses intimidation, manipulation, and often yelling and screaming to get his way. Passive people tend to keep everything inside and either agree with everything or attribute the problem to someone or something else.

Neither of these styles creates smooth sailing and often direct action is required in order to maintain a working relationship. One thing to remember is that you are really working with difficult *behaviors*, not difficult people. By focusing on the specific interaction patterns of the person whose actions you are seeking to modify, you enable them to change specific behaviors without feeling like they are "bad." From that perspective it is then possible to describe the situation to the person in a nonaccusatory manner, focusing on the exact behaviors. The next step is to describe the consequences stemming from this behavior. And, finally, state specifically and clearly what you want done to alter the behavior.

Going through these steps in detail will help you feel confident in using them. When you begin the meeting with someone whom you need to talk to because of difficult behavior, start off with a simple statement, not an accusation; you are seeking her cooperation. "I want very much to supervise an office where everyone is happy, so of course it's of concern to me whenever someone seems unhappy either with what she's doing or with the people she works with. When someone consistently abuses her co-workers it usually means that she's unhappy." Notice that the supervisor never made an accusation of it, in fact he never said "you," which might have made the person defensive. The comments were specific only as to the problem behavior. "Perhaps you can fill me in on what you feel some of your greatest difficulties to be. . . ."

Listening will be a very important part of this process. In fact in some cases it can alleviate the whole problem; she may have been difficult because she felt unnoticed, unappreciated, or unwanted. By listening you change her view of herself, of the company, and of you. When you listen to people who are on the more passive side you'll need to encourage them, to get a clear picture of what is bothering them. You'll also find yourself using active listening techniques—summarizing what you heard the other person say, and keeping on the subject. After the problem has been described and the listening phase completed, it's your turn to describe some of the consequences of the problem behavior. Sometimes it will come as a shock to the person to know that her behavior is having effects on company productivity, both in direct expenses and in morale. The third and final step is a clear, concise statement of what change is being asked. This is also the time to ask the person what changes she thinks are necessary and incorporate them into your statement. This makes it hard for her to feel that all changes were imposed on her unfairly, or that they're not good ideas. Make the suggestion as specific as possible, and include a time frame to reassess the person's progress. At the end of the session it is important to request a response and allow the person to make a commitment to change. If you get a noncommittal "maybe," then you need to go back through some of the original process to make it clear that what's at issue is not *whether* there's a problem, or *whether* it's going to be solved, but *how*. With people who are accustomed to intimidating others you may have to circle through this loop several times before a "no" changes to a "yes."

Some people will try to shift the focus. They will look hurriedly somewhere else for a place to fix the blame. Don't let the shifter shift. Tell her you'll deal with other people who are involved as needed but for now what you need is her cooperation and commitment.

In summary, dealing with difficult behaviors can be one of the hardest parts of working with others. The following list may come in handy:

1. Make the time of the discussion convenient
2. Be specific about the problem; use behavioral terms
3. Listen to the person carefully; use active listening skills
4. Don't accuse the person using words like "you"
5. Talk about behavior, things that can be changed, not attitudes
6. Don't expect an unreasonable amount of change in an unreasonably short time
7. Get a commitment to the plan

Part III

RENEWING YOURSELF

CHAPTER 6

Self-Renewal: Reconnecting with Yourself

Burnout often stems from a lack of awareness, consideration, and respect for our feelings, needs, values, and life goals. This chapter initiates a process of self-reflection, introducing exercises for learning about dimensions of ourselves that we neglect or that are simply out of everyday awareness. Whether we pay attention to these or not, they affect our lives. But when they lie outside of our awareness and consideration, we feel helpless and controlled by what we do and experience, and we miss opportunities to bring our lives into harmony with our internal needs, goals, and values.

People are not machines that can be pushed to high performance. When we push ourselves to accomplish something and we experience resistance, we need to ask ourselves why we are doing this, why it is important to us. Burnout and distress are sometimes a message from our bodies that we need to explore these basic questions. The symptoms signal not an inability to manage the outside world, but a disconnection within ourselves. So the processes of preventing and overcoming burnout and performing up to our capacities involve not only external management of difficult situations and working together with others, but also some inner reflection on such questions as who we are, what we need, and what we want from our lives. We also need to take proper care of ourselves—physically, emotionally, and spiritually—and replenish the energy we expend each day. These processes of going within and regenerating ourselves make up the activities that we call "self-renewal."

When the pressure of our lives reaches the point where we begin to notice signs of burnout, or when we reach a point of transition through a job loss or other life change, it is a good time for a reassessment of where we are, where we have come from, and where we are going. In the early 1960s management consultants like Herb Shepard began to offer executive seminars in "Life Planning." In these retreats the participants explored where they were in their lives and after reassessment, planned and executed changes. After these workshops executives reported positive changes in their personal lives and feelings about themselves, and in their performance at work. Through knowing where they were in life and where they might be going, they could reconnect in a more positive and creative way to their work. Others, of course, as a result of the workshop made important life changes—changing jobs, taking up new hobbies and activities, and reorienting their relationships. This chapter offers exercises from these and similar intensive workshops. You can work on them by yourself, or you can share the process with important people in your life.

Self-exploration and self-understanding are the cornerstones of self-renewal and are an antidote for burnout and excessive life stress. Unless we are self-aware, we are out of touch with important guidance concerning correct decisions and lack a sense of purpose and direction. In such a state even ordinary pressures and demands can confuse and immobilize us.

When we are feeling pressured or dissatisfied, it is a natural reflex to look around to try to discover the source of the stress. We look in the environment or in the people around us. There is an illusory sense of relief when we can blame our condition on something, even if the act of blaming leads us nowhere. Usually the reason that blaming leads us nowhere is that by looking outside us we neglect the one constant in every situation—ourselves.

The human being is composed of a vast inner conscious and unconscious world of often competing desires, feelings, thoughts, skills, goals, and expectations. Our rich capacity for self-awareness and our capacity to plan and act on our images and creative aspirations lead to the richness of human life and also to its pain and difficulty. Often the burnout we feel in a job is not due to the work situation itself, but to our idealistic expectations or our personal needs. Self-management begins not with control over the external world, but with an expansion of our awareness of our inner worlds.

This chapter explores some of the essential dimensions of your inner world: your conscious thoughts and feelings as well as memory of everything you have ever learned or experienced, and the goals, values, and desires that shape your behavior. The authors' purpose is to help you learn about the "you" that you bring into situations and how it may contribute to your distress. By exploring who we are, we gain access to our inner reserves, potential sources of strength, and capacities that can help us face life's demands and choose our future path wisely.

Many of the signs of burnout can be understood as messages that we are neglecting something within ourselves—a need or a feeling that our body is noticing. Much pressure comes from a disconnection or conflict in our relationship to ourselves. If there is disharmony, or we are not feeling good or at peace with ourselves, then it is difficult to manage the externals of work and life. At every stage of our lives we need to have at least provisional answers or working solutions to the deepest and most essential questions—who are we, what we want, where we are going, and what is most important to us. Only then can we make meaningful and satisfying choices about how to organize our life. The answers to these questions form the core of how we manage the pressures and demands of our lives.

WHO AM I: EXPLORING THE PERSON WITHIN

The Nature of the Person

Stress, distress, and burnout are all signs of conflict. Conflict can exist on many levels—between personal needs and the demands of the employer, between people, between groups of people, and between different factions within the self. For example, one of the major sources of personal stress is the way the organization treats individuals. Some organizations assume that people are interchangeable, that they need to be tightly controlled in order to perform, and that their feelings are irrelevant. These assumptions conflict with the way most of us experience ourselves. Stress, and later burnout, come about from trying to fit into the straitjacket of the organization's inadequate model of human nature.

We often buy these limited ideas about human nature and try to live by them. When we do this, we diminish ourselves and ignore essential facets of our complex nature. However, we usually don't succeed in treating ourselves like machines for long. Our body rebels, letting us know that we deserve better. We need to learn to listen to these messages.

Throughout this book the authors have been making certain assumptions about human nature. We assume that the person is a deeply complex and important being whose nature needs to be affirmed and validated in his or her life and work. In this chapter we begin by making these assumptions more explicit, and then help you to reflect on their relevance to you. Often burnout and distress have to do with difficulties in your understanding and respect for your inner self and potentialities. These assumptions are:

1. *Each person contains a vast inner world of thoughts, feelings, values, aspirations, potentials, and needs that he or she is capable of knowing and exploring. Distress, ill health, and burnout can result from neglecting this inner world.* We need to explore and connect to ourselves on this complex level, and to take this world into

account in all of our actions. Also, we need to act in reflection of these inner values, needs, and messages.

2. *Each person has a vast potential, which he or she rarely lives up to, and a complex and many-faceted nature.* Full and healthy living must respect our many facets, and reflect and express as many of our potentials as possible.

3. *People live in a world with others, and they need to feel connected, validated, helped, involved, and trusting in their relationships.* In order to get what we want and become who we want to be, we need to become deeply involved with others. People are communal, and solitary people seem to have difficulty with their health and well-being. Other people let us know of our value, and confirm and validate our sense of worth and identity. In order to feel safe in the world, we need to trust others.

4. *The person is continually changing, evolving, growing, and becoming.* Each of us is molded by past experience and habits, but we are ever changing. Much of our change is self-generated and self-created in the direction of our goals. We make choices every moment to act or not act, and we need to take responsibility for the direction we choose. People are not entirely molded by their environments or constraints, but always have the possibility of creative and novel choices and solutions to difficulties.

The picture of the person that we have painted is in sharp contrast to the now dated and clearly self-defeating image of man as a robot or machine. Indeed, many problems with stress and burnout seem to result from acting upon such limited conceptions of what people are. Curiously, while these limiting assumptions are often made by organizations, just as often we find that people feel that way about themselves or about other people. In many ways we neglect or limit ourselves by not being properly respectful or paying adequate attention to ourselves. In this chapter you will look more deeply and clearly at who you are, where you are going, and what you are capable of.

Personal Needs

There are many things a human being needs to remain alive. This includes air, food, and shelter. But in order to grow and thrive a person needs much more. People need other people for companionship, for love, and for personal support. People also have psychological needs, which include establishing and maintaining self-esteem, a feeling of being valued, a need to be competent, challenge, achievement, intense experience, transcendent and spiritual connections and finding meaning and purpose in living.

Psychologist Abraham Maslow suggested that not all people feel all needs with the same urgency at the same time. Maslow proposed that at certain times of one's life certain needs were paramount. For example, a young person might be most concerned about a lack of a deep intimate relationship and less focused on other needs. Maslow also observed that many basic needs seemed to be met for most people, and that as these needs were met, other types of needs—for such things as personal growth and creative self-expression—became important. For example, since most of us have enough to eat, food is rarely a concern for us. In a poor country concern about bare physical survival is paramount.

The needs for other people, for achievement, and for a meaningful life seem to be most important for people today. These are the needs that are unmet, or inadequately met, for many people. When some basic needs are frustrated, the body usually responds with the psychophysiological stress response. Over time, with continual frustration, stress builds up and various physical and emotional difficulties arise.

Because frustration of basic needs is one of the messages of burnout and stress, we begin our internal self-exploration with an inquiry into your experience of what needs are most central to you right now, and how well they are satisfied.

Self-Esteem

One central human need is for self-esteem, to experience ourselves positively, to feel competent and effective at what we do, to feel cared for and valued, and to feel good about who we are. When we feel good about ourselves, we act differently than we do when we feel threatened, disliked, and unvalued. When we have high self-esteem, we feel good, confident, and creative. The cultivation and enhancement of self-esteem is therefore necessary for our well-being.

Self-esteem is not something we have or don't have. Even though people who grow up in a family where they feel loved and accepted for who they are have an easier time maintaining positive feelings for themselves than people with a more frustrating or deprived background, still, self-esteem is something that can be developed. We can create situations and act in such a way that it grows and flourishes.

There are several sources of self-esteem: achievements; power and influence over events and people; feeling accepted, valued, and cared for by people we value; and acting consistently with personal values.

The reverse is also true. Self-esteem declines when we do not act, when we abdicate our personal power, when we do not connect to the people around us, and when we do not articulate and act on our core values and beliefs. The sources of self-esteem are almost identical to

(text continues on page 133)

E X E R C I S E 15

NEEDS ASSESSMENT

Listed below are some of the important personal needs. For each type of need indicate how important or pressing it is for you, and how satisfied you are in that area in your current life. If you are not feeling satisfied in some areas, you may be experiencing stress.

Type of Need	Importance Lo Med Hi	Satisfaction Lo Med Hi
Sexuality		
Friendship		
Being Loved		
Loving Others		
Self-Esteem		
Creative Achievement		
Religious Experience, Spirituality		
Respect of Peers		
Excitement, Challenge		
Quiet, Peacefulness		

the activities that help you manage your life, overcome stress and burnout, and achieve personal effectiveness.

Consider to what degree each of the potential sources of self-esteem are operative in your life now. For each source ask yourself if you enhance your self-esteem in that way. Your sense of self-esteem will probably derive more from one or two of the areas. Also, think about the different spheres of your life—work, family, friends, and you alone. Which sources of self-esteem are experienced in each one? For example, do you derive your sense of acceptance more from your family, and experience power and achievement in your work?

Open and Defensive Behavior

It is interesting to think about our encounters with other people in terms of self-esteem. Every interaction has some effect on the self-esteem of the people involved. Many of our interactions are even intended to support our self-esteem. For example, we like to be seen positively, so we avoid offending other people and sometimes even avoid telling them bad news or being honest about mistakes we have made. Most people tend to blame circumstances or other people for mistakes, which is partly an attempt to salvage self-esteem.

When we look at interaction in terms of self-esteem, we can see two intentions that lie behind our behavior. We can relate defensively —acting primarily to protect our feelings of self-worth from real or imagined harm—or openly—sharing our true feelings and being open to those of the other person. In every interaction we can sense to what degree we are open or defensive. When we see ourselves acting defensively, we need to look at what we are trying to protect ourselves from. Many times we are defending ourselves from a threat that is more imagined than real.

People work best when the people around them validate their value and worth. When people around us support our self-esteem, we feel more trust and become more open and effective. Much of the stress and burnout that occur in work settings (and in families) stem from interactions that do not validate self-esteem.

Defensive settings are ineffective, both at getting work done and in supporting personal well-being. Here is what happens. People do not support each other's positive worth. They criticize, backbite, and withhold compliments. Each person feels bad and becomes more defensive—withholding important information, covering up problems and mistakes, and avoiding responsibility. Over time people begin to feel more powerless, unsupported, lonely, and frustrated. Things get worse and worse.

Another outcome results when one key person in a work group begins to set up interactions that validate and support people's self-esteem. The person who supports others gets better responses from the people nearby, who in turn feel better and do better work. Trust
(text continues on page 135)

E X E R C I S E 16

WHO AM I?

Write as many answers to this question as you can, but not fewer than twenty. You can list roles, feelings, things you like to do, qualities that reflect essential aspects of yourself. Be wide ranging.

1. _____
2. _____
3. _____
4. _____
5. _____
6. _____
7. _____
8. _____
9. _____
10. _____
11. _____
12. _____
13. _____
14. _____
15. _____
16. _____
17. _____
18. _____
19. _____
20. _____
21. _____
22. _____
23. _____
24. _____
25. _____

builds and people begin to be more supportive and validating of each other.

Exercise 16 explores your personal sense of identity. Take some time and complete the list of answers to the question, "Who am I?" Look at the list. Notice how no single definition or answer encompasses the whole of you. And also be aware that the whole of you is much more than even all the answers on the page. You are much more than that. Go over your list of answers again, and remember the answers in terms of those most important to you. Which touch closest to the core of who you are? Which are less important? Finally, look at each answer, beginning with the most important, and think of where, how, and when you express this quality or aspect of yourself, and then think up some other ways that you can express it. Write these down.

The degree to which a setting supports the self-esteem of the people in it is critical to personal self-worth and also to its effectiveness. Things that support people's sense of worth and psychological well-being also encourage health and optimal performance.

Exploring Ourselves

We can think of each aspect of ourself and our personality as a different self. That is, we can take a quality or facet and explore it as if it is a being that lives within us. Instead of seeing ourself as a single, unified whole, it is more realistic to think of ourself as a kind of loose confederation of different selves, each with its own place and purpose. Philosopher James Ogilvy and psychiatrist Robert Jay Lifton both point out that instead of looking for a single core identity, people today need to see themselves as what Lifton calls "protean," many-faceted, many-identitied people who are in flux and developing in new ways. Today we can expect to change jobs several times in our lives, and even to be in different intimate relationships, living in different places, and have a variety of involvements and interests.

One way to divide up our different identities is through different aspects of conscious experience. We have several modes for experiencing ourselves and the world. These modes include body sensing, thinking, feeling, and action. Take a moment now to turn your attention inward and see that you have direct sensation from your body, that you are also having thoughts and feelings, and that you can act and experience your behavior and its consequences.

Think about how and where you experience each of the selves that lie within you. Which of them are more familiar to you? Which are less often used? How can you explore your body self, your thinking self, your feeling self, and your action self? Think of different aspects of your daily life. When does each of these selves come into play? Which ones might you consult more frequently, or look at more? For many of us, especially those who face stress-related problems, difficulties stem from neglect of our body self, or feeling self. Think of ways to pay more attention to the facets of yourself you are neglecting.

Pressure, distress, dissatisfaction, and burnout can often result from a life that reflects only a narrow slice of who you are. For example, a person who has a routine job and who has a rich family life, or a variety of community involvement, or a complex and demanding hobby, will probably experience less burnout and dissatisfaction on that job than a person who has very little to look forward to when he or she leaves work. The more of ourself that we express, and the more that we express our many qualities and potentials, the less frustrated and burned out we will be.

Think back over your life and remember things that you have done, things that you sometime thought you'd like to do, things that you have stopped doing, things you have never done. Remember how you felt doing those things, or how much you wanted to do them. Ask yourself why you didn't do them, or stopped doing them. You may think, I don't have time for them, or I don't know anybody to do them with, or some similar excuse. Now imagine how your life would be enriched and broadened by including some of these activities. List several activities that you might begin doing.

There are difficulties involved in actualizing our multifaceted nature. Life does not become richer just because we do more things. We need to find balance and make choices about what to express and act on. Time and life are finite, and our interests and possibilities are infinite. We need to make choices and set limits.

Some of the conflict in our lives is caused by differences between the actual and the possible, between the way we appear and the way we are. When these differences are too great, the gaps can be a source of distress. Below is a list of some of the types of difference that lead to conflict. On each side of the page list a few phrases that describe yourself along that dimension:

Me at Work ⟷ *Me at Home*
The Roles I Play ⟷ *The Person I Really Am*
How Others See Me ⟷ *How I See Myself*
How I Am ⟷ *How I'd Like to Be*

As you look at the differences along these dimensions, imagine what it would feel like if each of these areas was more congruent. What steps could you take to make yourself more integrated? Are these changes worth it to you?

Myths and Roles

Many people create stress by unrealistic expectations of themselves. We expect ourselves to accomplish the impossible. A person may be evaluating his or her behavior in terms of "shoulds." For example, he may say that a good employee should always finish all the work he is assigned, or a good husband should always be ready to help out around the house, or a friend should always be available to help a person who is upset. The myth of what an employee, boss, parent, spouse, or friend should be leads us to expect more than we have, or leads us to criticize our efforts as inadequate.

Write down your major roles or identities—at work, in family, or in the community. For each role write down some of the things that you expect yourself to do in that position. Now ask yourself if these are what you expect of yourself in these roles. And, if you fall short, what do you say or do to yourself? Much of our daily stress comes from not living up to our expectations. Usually we expect much more from ourselves than the people in our work site or family expect of us.

MOVING THROUGH LIFE: THE PERSON IN PROCESS

The Lifeline

We live in the present, yet at this moment we are the total of all the events and experiences of our past, and are also determined by our vision of our future and our hopes and goals. The first exercise in self-exploration and life planning is to step back from the present and look at your life as an evolving whole.

Your lifeline is shown below. The left edge represents your birth, and the right edge your death. In between is the "now" line. Draw your lifeline as follows, in pencil (so you can make changes): write in the significant events in your life—important changes, transitions, crises, moves, illnesses—in the interval between your birth and today. Write the positive or exciting events toward the top of the chart and the stressful or negative events toward the bottom edge. You are entering the highs and lows and changes in your life so far. Include not only events happening to you, but significant events in your family and, if you wish, significant social/political events. Now draw a line connecting the events, moving up and down, to represent the emotional climate and progression of your life. Next, try to divide your life into a series of phases or periods that make sense to you. For example, your college education, your first marriage, job, or time living in one place. (There is a sample lifeline on p. 139 to illustrate.)

Next envision possible futures. Fill in the one you would like to see between the "now" line and your death with hypothetical significant events. Continue your lifeline, projecting yourself into the future.

All lifelines are different—they're shaped by different events and actions or decisions. How many of the actions that shaped your lifeline resulted from choices you made, and how many from choices others

YOUR LIFELINE

BIRTH	NOW	DEATH

made for you? Is there evidence of action you've taken without really making a decision, that is, something you did simply because it was expected of you?

Put the following symbols along your lifeline. Put ! where you took the greatest risk. Place X where you encountered an obstacle preventing you from getting or doing what you wanted. Use O to locate a critical decision that was made for you by someone else. Put + at the point of the best decision you ever made and − at the worst decision you made. Finally put ? where you see a critical or important decision coming up in the future.

Consider your lifeline carefully now, complete with symbols.

Have you learned anything that surprises you?_____

_____

_____

How have decisions affected the shape of your lifeline?_____

_____

_____

Did you actually make the decisions that affected your life?_____

_____

_____

SAMPLE LIFELINE

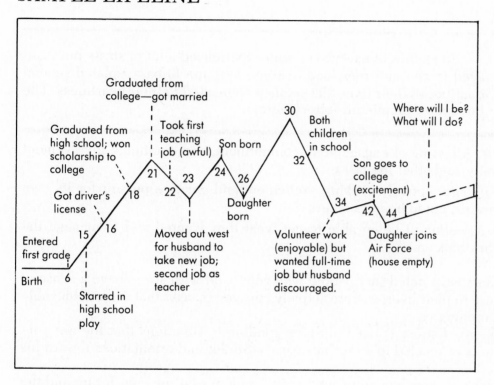

Life Goals

Imagine facing a difficult and stressful situation in a job or family that is important and meaningful to you. Whatever the situation, you will probably find the energy to face the problem and do your best to resolve it. Now imagine you have a job or live with people whose general welfare or goals do not coincide with yours. The struggle with the stressful situation will be that much greater.

The phenomenon of burnout has several roots. One is the extent to which the place you work, or the people you live with, share your goals. Second, there is the degree to which you feel that you can actively pursue those goals. Do you feel a sense of power?

One of the primary causes of burnout and inability to manage stress is working or living in a setting without clear goals or feeling able to meet your goals. A situation is supportive when all the people working or living there have a large area of shared commitments and goals, and when all the people are involved in them. When individual

(text continues on page 142)

139

E X E R C I S E   17

SELF-ASSESSMENT: MEANING AND LIFE PURPOSE

In studies of executives who experienced a lot of stress but managed it well and remained healthy, Suzanne Kobasa isolated several qualities of their lives that seemed connected to their heartiness. The three most prominent factors were:

- *Involvement:* A feeling of engagement, commitment, and emotional involvement in work, family, and other life tasks
- *Seeking challenge:* Actively seeking excitement and creative pursuit for its own intrinsic rewards, not to impress others
- *In control:* A feeling of being able to get what they wanted and to manage the situations they took on

Other researchers have noted that people who cope well with stress have a sense of meaning and purpose in their lives, and are actively engaged in tasks that seem achievable and relevant to their energies.

Thus management of stress is not simply responding to situations that the environment serves up, but is connected to a person's basic attitudes and orientations toward his or her life.

This exercise looks at how you approach living, and how you see your future and the meaningfulness of your life, work, and relationships.

For each statement indicate the degree to which you agree or disagree.

	Strongly Agree	Agree	Disagree	Strongly Disagree
1. I am not involved in my work	3	2	1	0
2. My work is not very meaningful or satisfying to me	3	2	1	0
3. My work feels routine and boring	3	2	1	0
4. There are few challenges and creative tasks in my work	3	2	1	0
5. I am not very involved with my family	3	2	1	0
6. My family life is not very satisfying or meaningful to me	3	2	1	0
7. I am bored and disinterested in my family life	3	2	1	0
8. My life is rarely challenging and exciting	3	2	1	0
9. Nothing much is new or unpredictable in my life	3	2	1	0
10. My life does not have a central purpose or goal	3	2	1	0
11. My life does not seem to meet many of my deepest needs	3	2	1	0
12. My life is taken up with burdens and responsibilities	3	2	1	0
13. There is not much that I look forward to in my life	3	2	1	0
14. I do not feel that there is any higher force or guiding purpose evident in humanity	3	2	1	0
15. I do not feel that I have lived up to my potential or lived as creatively and successfully as I might have	3	2	1	0
TOTAL				

If you score more than 25 on this scale, you are experiencing considerable difficulty in feeling connected to your life and meeting your personal needs. Scores between 15 and 24 indicate moderate problems which suggest you need to explore more clearly what you want from your life and why you have not been able to get it.

goals are far away from the group goals (for example, people are working only for their salaries, not caring about what the organization produces), burnout and added stress result and it is harder to marshal the energy to overcome difficulties.

Think about your life goals and how supportive your work and home environments are to those goals. Many times we are not even conscious of having life goals, or something to work toward. Without goals the struggle to overcome difficulties has no point. Having a meaningful future makes the stress of the present worth overcoming.

Some people who do have life goals do not feel they have the power to achieve them, or they feel blocked by their environment. Sometimes if we cannot achieve our goals in one setting, we must make the decision to leave and try another place. Other times we must take risks to make changes. Some risks succeed, some fail. However, when we feel helpless and do not make changes to achieve our goals, the resulting stagnation produces great stress, and burnout.

Think about the major obstacles to achieving your goals in each area of your life. What risks could you take to make them happen? What fears do you have about taking these risks? Inability to formulate and work toward personal goals creates stress because it robs a person of a reason to overcome challenges and deal with frustration. The more meaningful the goal, the more life energy and support a person can muster to overcome difficulty.

Play and Pleasure.   People who know how to play and have fun are more relaxed and better able to bounce back from stressful situations. The guiding principle of effective stress management seems to be balance. People need to balance work and play, sleep and wakefulness, stress and relaxation, activity and rest. Therefore, one of the best antidotes to a stressful day is play.

Observe a child. Moving spontaneously, laughing and finding pleasure, and showing very little anxiety or muscle tension, the child is a picture of adaptive stress management. The child has much to teach us.

How many times a day do you laugh, not snicker or chuckle, but let your whole body give in to laughter? How playful are you in your personal relationships? Can you let down your guard and respond playfully to things? Play is one of the most effective ways to manage and release the buildup of daily tension.

Work and Family

The greatest and most difficult conflicts many of us will ever experience are those between work and family. These take two forms: first we have to divide our priorities, commitments, time, and energy between work and family/personal involvements; second, there are

(text continues on page 147)

E X E R C I S E 18

PERSONAL GOAL INVENTORY

In each area of your life what are your major, concrete, specific goals? Try to be concrete. Don't think about how you want to feel (e.g., happy, challenged), but what you want to happen in the next few years and how it could come about. Relax and imagine a future in which, over the next few years, you are working toward your goals. The more details you can imagine in your future, the more likely you are to discover ways to bring it about.

Next, think of the major obstacles to realizing your goals. Often they lie within the setting, or you experience resistance from people around you. Think clearly about the specific obstacles to realizing what you want. Finally, imagine several concrete, immediate, active steps you can take to empower yourself and to begin to work actively to overcome the obstacles. Be concrete and specific.

Write these thoughts on the chart.

Area of Life	Specific Goals	Obstacles to Achieving Them	Steps to Be Taken to Achieve
Current Job			
Career			
Family			
Friendships			
Spiritual/Religious			
Play			
Personal Growth			
Community/Political			
Other Areas			

E X E R C I S E 19

EXPLORING YOUR ENERGY COMMITMENTS

Consider how you allocate your time and energy among the different areas of your life. In the graph below indicate the amount of energy and time you give to work, play, relationships to friends and family, and to yourself.

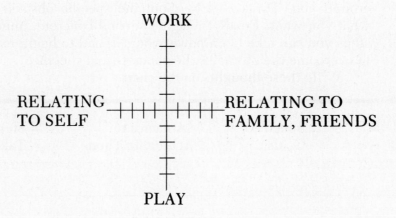

Now indicate how much energy you would like to devote to each of these areas.

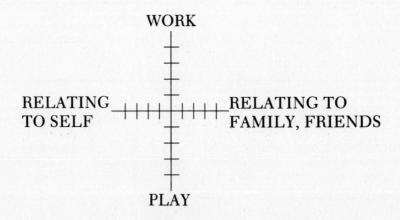

Write down some of the activities you do in each domain of your life. Then add some of the ones you would like to do or think you might want to do.

_____
_____
_____
_____
_____
_____

_____
_____

WORK

SELF **OTHERS**

PLAY

_____
_____
_____
_____
_____
_____
_____

E X E R C I S E 20

ENERGY BALANCE

The essential concept of self-care is balance. Our various needs must be balanced, and our own needs must balance with those of others.

Like any organism the human being is a system that exchanges energy with its environment. We take in various forms of energy—air, food, experience, and contact with others—and we also give energy out—exhalation, excretion, communication, action, and personal support.

In looking at our energy balance, we need to explore the various modes of action we engage in. Activity differs in terms of the source of motivation and also the direction it takes. The source can be *intrinsic*, doing things because we want to, or *extrinsic*, doing things because we feel we should, or ought to, or have to do them. The direction of activity can be *giving*, doing things for others, or *receiving*, allowing others to do things for and to us. None of these modes is in itself right or wrong, or healthy or unhealthy. Rather, people who feel good about themselves and manage stress well have a balance of energy in each area.

In the Energy Balance exercise fill in your regular activities in the appropriate quadrant. See which areas predominate in your life, and which are less usual.

Receiving	Intrinsic
Things done to and for you by others	Things you do because you want to

Extrinsic	Giving
Things you do because you "should," "have to," or "ought to"	Things you do to and for others

conflicts between members of a household, especially a couple's differing levels of commitment to work or family.

Any conflict causes pressure and distress. Often we can't find a way to make ourselves fully satisfied, or to satisfy ourselves and our spouse. Added to this, recent changes in sex roles, such as the restructuring of household expectations, parental responsibilities, and women entering previously male-dominated work settings, have required even old agreements and solutions to be renegotiated.

One of the most difficult conflicts is finding enough time and energy to do everything we want. Work can eat up our time and energy, sometimes leaving us with little left over for our family. Tragically, working people too often make their family and personal relationships their lowest priority, giving them what, if anything, is left over. Yet people who are successful at managing stress and remaining healthy are often those who make their personal and family lives a priority and are able to say "no" to some outside demands. Setting priorities to give importance to both work and family is a cornerstone of a balanced life and self-renewal.

The other area of conflict, often more severe, is between two people in a couple. Each has a different interpretation or need for time together, and each has differing priorities. Balancing two careers, or finding time to be together when one is on the "fast-track" at work, is difficult. Couples that solve these dilemmas are clear and open about each other's needs and commitments, share information and feelings, and are flexible in compromising or looking for something other than win/lose solutions.

Current Life Exploration

As part of your life planning and self-renewal process, explore where you are right now, and look ahead at some choices and changes that you might want to make. Exercises 17–20 as well as the following questions are guides for your reflections on your current life situation. Jot down some of your thoughts on each theme (you don't need to have a complete answer; life is continually changing). The purpose is to make your feelings about your life more explicit, and to define some areas and dimensions of life that need renewed energy or redefined commitment.

1. What are my current concerns and worries?
2. What are the greatest pressures on me right now? When do I feel it? What must I do about it?
3. What is changing in my life?
4. What are the major values or goals that I would like to achieve in my life?

5. What are the most important payoffs or rewards that I am looking for in my life?

6. What intense, gratifying, and deeply meaningful experiences have I had in my life? What sorts of peak experiences would I like to have in the future?

7. What are the major constraints or limits that I experience in my life right now, which make it difficult to achieve the rewards, goals, and experiences I seek?

8. What are the major obstacles to getting what I want out of life? (Divide them into obstacles that lie inside you and those which are external. Think of some of the ways you can change or diminish the force of these obstacles.)

9. What are the things I do well? List them.

10. What are the things that I do poorly? Would I like to improve my ability in these areas or stop doing these things?

11. What would I like to stop doing?

12. What would I like to start doing or learn to do?

13. What are the central goals in my life right now? What were my goals five years ago? What do I project will be my goals five years from now?

14. Which of the things that I do regularly do I expect to do less often in the following years? What new things do I expect to have to do, or want to do?

15. What is the most important change or crisis that I expect to face in the next decade?

16. What is the most important choice I will have to make in the next few years?

17. Which domain of my life (work, family, friends, self) is the central one right now? In the next five years which domains do I expect to become more and less important in my life?

18. What ideal futures can I anticipate? (Imagine what you would like to experience, what you would like to be doing, and who or what kind of people you would like to be doing things with.)

19. Imagine at some time in the future you have just died. Write your obituary as the person in your life closest to you might write it. What do you expect you will be remembered for? What sort of achievements do you expect to have?

Career Exploration

1. What facets of my career do I enjoy most or find most meaningful?

2. What facets of my career do I like least?

3. Where in my work do I find the greatest challenge?

4. What skills, talents, and abilities do I bring to my job?

5. What skills, talents, and abilities could my work potentially allow me to develop?

6. What do I want out of my work, what benefits and rewards?

7. What led me to choose the type of work I do? What values and personal feelings led me to this type of work?

8. How has my work been unsatisfying, or how has my satisfaction with my work diminished?

9. What new areas, skills, and types of work would I like to pursue? What prevents me from going in one of these directions?

10. What is the greatest frustration and difficulty in my work? What would I most like to change about my work?

Creating Change in Your Life

The explorations in this chapter have produced a wealth of information for you about where you are in your life and who you are as a person. You will have spent many hours reflecting on the questions and you have probably ended up with a much deeper view of yourself and your life. You will be particularly aware of your deepest satisfactions and needs, and of several areas of your life that are in need of change.

There is no simple set of instructions for proceeding with a personal change process. Some people can reflect and then begin to plan and implement changes. Others work with the people closest to them —family and friends—to create changes. Still others vacillate back and forth, either because they are not clear what to change or they cannot find the energy to motivate them to begin.

Our philosophy is that change represents a very deep commitment and consequential decision. It should not be done impulsively or initiated too quickly. First you must select an area of your life in which you would like to see change. Then spend time, as you have done in several other areas already, imagining concretely and specifically alternative possibilities. When you envision concretely, you begin to see consequences and have the opportunity to experience what the projected change would be like in your life. Many times the envisioning process helps you see unintended consequences, or lack of clarity in your decision or plan.

The generation of alternate possibilities and directions, a sort of list of possible pathways, is critical to change. Often, merely setting ourselves free from the way things are now and envisioning or thinking about how things can be different, is a highly creative act. We see things that we never looked at before. As you generate alternatives, just let them come up without criticism. When you have a large list of possibilities, try to explore their possible consequences and results. Very often this portion of planning and changing can be done best with the people closest to you.

The methods of change are up to you. Many people use personal counseling or psychotherapy. Many of the exercises and techniques in this book are derived from therapeutic processes. The newer styles of psychotherapy are not based on seeing people as mentally ill or deficient; rather they espouse the growth model of human potential outlined at the start of this chapter, which sees counseling as personal guidance to help people reach their unique potential and creativity.

But change does not require counseling or therapy. It requires a clear decision and a personal will to take risks and attempt new behavior. It often involves practicing new skills and learning new methods of response, as you have done in this book. But given the range of possibilities and the shifting demands of our lives, a person who does not welcome change and learn new things will be seriously handicapped.

CHAPTER 7

Attunement: Skills for Attaining Relaxation and Physical Wellness

Many people don't discover that they are burned out until they become physically ill, or until the self-defeating ways they use to manage stress—such as drinking or eating—cause them serious harm. Then the same people who are adept at managing their outside worlds become incapable of renewing their bodies. Their skills stop with their skin, and they feel helpless to battle self-destructive habits of managing tension. As things build up, the damage becomes more and more irreversible.

The body, like any organization, is a self-regulating system. Both physical and organizational systems have boundaries with the outside world, and have internal processes that manage the flow of materials, resources, services, and information. Both systems develop, growing more complex over time, and are continually threatened by change. Either a person or an organization can act self-destructively, causing damage by ineffective action, and perhaps die. Both types of systems need to grow and develop while at the same time maintaining and renewing themselves.

The key to self-renewing, whether within an organization or within a person, lies in the level of awareness of threats, and the strategies for dealing with them. Organisms must be vigilant and take care of themselves. Physiologically, this means taking care of all physical systems, replenishing them with rest and reenergizing them, exchanging energy and resources with others, and becoming aware of difficulty early enough to exercise corrective reaction. While many people know how to do these things organizationally—using strategic planning, market research and quality control to remain aware—they do not exercise the same care and awareness when it comes to their bodies.

If we are not aware of small fluctuations in a system, they grow. Consider, for example, the buildup of muscle tension when under stress. Muscles become chronically tense over a day, and we become less and less sensitive to this tension. Then we go home and move something that would ordinarily be manageable, and we accidentally strain our back. Was the strain caused by moving the table, or by lack of awareness and lack of corrective response to release the growing tension?

We need to heed the messages of our body in order to maintain health and our natural physiological resources to resist stress, overcome burnout, and prevent illness. Stress and burnout are our major health problems, and because, as we are learning, we can manage stress without damage to ourselves, these health problems are largely preventable.

The first line of defense against the physical symptoms caused by stress is effective regular care of the body. The body must be kept flexible, rested, responsive, energized, aware of itself, and prepared to meet demands. This means getting enough sleep, eating well, exercising, and releasing the tension that builds up each day through relaxation techniques. This chapter shows how stress and tension are taking root in your body, and teaches you specific techniques to bring your body back to the state of readiness to meet new demands. It also presents an introduction to the new orientation taking place in medicine and health care, known as "wellness training."

The first part of this chapter assesses the effects of stress and tension on your body. Then there is a brief introduction to wellness, and how to increase your self-awareness of your physical state. The second part offers some basic methods to attain relaxation, and offers ways to integrate relaxation practice into your active daily life.

WELLNESS, ILLNESS, AND TENSION

The Search for Wellness

A healthy, vital, creative, and fulfilling life is within our grasp. How do we remain healthy? The first thought many people have is medical insurance. If we become ill, we want to be certain that the most modern, up-to-date medical expertise and technology are available to us. And we want to be sure that saving our life will not ruin our prosperity and family's economic future.

As we reflect further on our health, we see that being healthy is much more than simply the absence of illness. Health involves a feeling of vitality, of energy, of ability to do what we want to do, of involvement in meaningful activity. In short, "health" involves the entire quality of our life.

The question facing each of us is how much is our health within our control. Is health, or prosperity, or wisdom, a matter of chance or factors beyond our control? No. Your health is up to you.

The language of warfare is used to describe disease. We are "invaded" by viruses, or our hearts are "attacked." For many people the enemy of health is labeled "stress," the daily invasion of demands, frustrations, changes, overstimulation, and pressure. The factors that cause disease are popularly thought to be powerful, overwhelming, insidious, and almost irresistible.

Our own power to resist or overcome disease is ignored or neglected. We speak of disease "victims," suggesting that those who become ill are innocent and defenseless. Only with the help of physicians and hospitals can the puny individual make any headway against the forces of disease.

While it may be true that our body is to some extent a battleground for opposing forces, more often than not we weaken ourselves by undermining our ability to resist disease, and by carelessly ignoring the dangers that face us.

The truth is that most disease is preventable, and most life stress is manageable. The pain, heart disease, ulcers, and even cancer that ruin our lives, threaten our livelihoods, and eventually kill us are often unnecessary. While we may still die of a heart attack or cancer, evidence is growing that we can postpone that death, or bring it upon ourselves much earlier than nature may have intended. Health or illness is a choice that each person makes.

Working for Wellness

The term "wellness" is new. It was coined in 1973 by physician John Travis, who founded a Wellness Resource Center outside San Francisco. If you aren't sick in bed, most people would say you are healthy. However, optimal living is more than that. High-level wellness, to Travis, is a state of active well-being where a person is actively engaged in taking care of himself, feeling good about his relationship to others and himself, and feeling involved, vital, alive, and creative. Working toward wellness begins when you are healthy, or free of symptoms.

An active wellness program is a commitment to work toward health. It involves learning to take better care of yourself, changing negative and self-destructive health habits, and looking at difficulties and problems in your life. Maintaining health and preventing disease demand careful thought about the way we live our lives, and learning new skills to manage everyday demands.

Traditional medicine works with diseases and helps us to overcome physical symptoms and crises. Wellness medicine is an educational program in which we become active participants in the process.

(text continues on page 157)

E X E R C I S E 21

ASSESSING YOUR OWN WELLNESS

Thinking not only about the presence or absence of a specific disease, how would you rate your overall level of wellness, your state of vitality, health, and well-being?

LOW   1   2   3   4   5   6   7   HIGH
POOR   EXCELLENT

Reflect on the things in your life that prevent you from being as well as you would like, the obstacles to optimal health. List at least five of them, beginning with the ones that most inhibit your health.

1.

2.

3.

4.

5.

Look over your list and think about the degree to which these obstacles to greater health and well-being are within your control. That is, are there things that you could do to prevent them from doing damage, or eliminate them from your life? Circle the items on your list that you feel could be changed or overcome.

EXERCISE 22

PERSONAL WELLNESS CHECKLIST

To estimate your degree of wellness, check how often each of the following is true for you.

	Almost Always	Often	Sometimes	Almost Never
1. I awake each morning feeling refreshed and energetic	3	2	1	0
2. I feel that I can get what I want out of life	3	2	1	0
3. I enjoy my family relationships	3	2	1	0
4. I know that other people care about me	3	2	1	0
5. My body is flexible and full of energy	3	2	1	0
6. I enjoy regular exercise	3	2	1	0
7. I eat nutritious and well-balanced meals	3	2	1	0
8. I have good, reliable friendships	3	2	1	0
9. There are people in whom I can confide	3	2	1	0
10. I like the way my life is going	3	2	1	0
11. I am working toward my life goals	3	2	1	0
12. I am able to manage the stress in my life	3	2	1	0
13. I am involved in my work, and find it meaningful	3	2	1	0
14. I do not smoke	3	2	1	0
15. I avoid overuse of alcohol and drugs	3	2	1	0
16. I know how to have fun	3	2	1	0

	Almost Always	Often	Sometimes	Almost Never
17. My body is a source of pleasure to me	3	2	1	0
18. I take good care of my teeth and the rest of my body	3	2	1	0
19. I express my creative and spiritual selves	3	2	1	0
20. I know that I can get what I need from others	3	2	1	0
TOTAL				

Scores can range from 0 to 60.

A score over 45 indicates a high degree of wellness.

A score between 30 and 45 indicates that you exercise self-care and experience wellness in some areas of your life, but need to make changes in some of your activities.

A score between 15 and 30 indicates that you are not experiencing much wellness in your life. You need to begin a health promotion program at once.

A score below 15 indicates serious difficulties in your life, demanding immediate attention.

There is no reason to settle for a score below 50. While there are difficulties, demands, and frustrations in any life, everyone has the capacity to manage her difficulties, develop good relationships and feelings about herself, and experience high-level wellness.

Only a wellness program can help us prevent future illnesses and preserve our body and well-being.

Symptoms of Stress

It is easy to know when we are under too much stress. Minor symptoms like headaches, insomnia, bowel difficulties or muscle tension are signals that pressures have built up to dangerously high levels. Sometimes such symptoms are a response to unusual demands and crises that are soon over—a deadline, an examination, a new job, a family conflict. However, many people experience so much daily tension that the common stress symptoms become almost a way of life. They are plagued by physical symptoms or emotional distress on a regular basis, perhaps every day. If these symptoms are not taken care of, more serious illness will develop as the body gradually wears down under the pressure.

Exercise 23 lists common physical and emotional symptoms that are partially due to ineffective coping with stress. Think back over the past month, and how frequently you have experienced each symptom. If you find that you have a number of symptoms as frequently as every week, you need to do something about them. Of course, it is important to note that while these symptoms are commonly associated with excessive stress, the presence of a symptom can also indicate some specific illness that may have relatively little to do with your life stress. So if you have a chronic physical·or emotional symptom, you need to have it checked out by a doctor.

Having stress-related symptoms is a message from your body that you are not managing the pressure and demands of your life well enough. The symptoms are the end point of a long chain of events that have to do with the demands made upon you, your thoughts and feelings about them, and the way you respond to them.

No matter what the particular symptom that causes you distress, its presence suggests that you need to learn regular relaxation. The techniques in this chapter will help you to manage your life so that physical and emotional distress are less likely to accumulate.

Your Relationship to Your Body

When we allow stress to build up, we demonstrate that we are out of touch with our bodies. Pain can be thought of as the body shouting for attention because we didn't pay attention to previous gentle signals of pressure or fatigue. Pain is the insistence that we pay attention to our own needs.

How do you feel about your body? Do you like it, dislike it, or not think about it very much? How much attention and care do you give your body? Is your body a friend or an enemy, a source of pleasure or

(*text continues on page 162*)

EXERCISE 23

STRESS SYMPTOMS CHECKLIST

Check how frequently you have experienced each of the following symptoms of distress over the past month. Total your scores.

I. Musculoskeletal System	Nearly Every Day	Every Week	Once or Twice	Never
1. Muscle tension	3	2	1	0
2. Back pain	3	2	1	0
3. Headaches	3	2	1	0
4. Grinding Teeth	3	2	1	0
II. Gastrointestinal System				
5. Stomachache or upset	3	2	1	0
6. Heartburn	3	2	1	0
7. Vomiting	3	2	1	0
8. Diarrhea	3	2	1	0
9. Constipation	3	2	1	0
10. Abdominal pains	3	2	1	0

III. Other Physical Systems	Nearly Every Day	Every Week	Once or Twice	Never
11. Colds, allergies	3	2	1	0
12. Chest pains	3	2	1	0
13. Skin rashes	3	2	1	0
14. Dry mouth	3	2	1	0
15. Laryngitis	3	2	1	0
16. Palpitations	3	2	1	0
IV. Tension/Anxiety				
17. Tremors or trembling	3	2	1	0
18. Twitches or tics	3	2	1	0
19. Dizziness	3	2	1	0
20. Nervousness	3	2	1	0
21. Anxiety	3	2	1	0
22. Tension and jitteriness	3	2	1	0
23. Keyed-up feeling	3	2	1	0
24. Worrying	3	2	1	0
25. Unable to keep still	3	2	1	0
26. Fear of certain objects, phobias	3	2	1	0
V. Energy Level				
27. Fatigue	3	2	1	0
28. Low energy	3	2	1	0
29. Apathetic, nothing seems important	3	2	1	0

VI. Depression	Nearly Every Day	Every Week	Once or Twice	Never
30. Depression	3	2	1	0
31. Fearfulness	3	2	1	0
32. Hopelessness	3	2	1	0
33. Crying easily	3	2	1	0
34. Highly self-critical	3	2	1	0
35. Frustrated	3	2	1	0
VII. Sleep				
36. Insomnia	3	2	1	0
37. Difficulty awakening	3	2	1	0
38. Nightmares	3	2	1	0
VIII. Attention				
39. Accidents or injuries	3	2	1	0
40. Difficulty concentrating	3	2	1	0
41. Mind going blank	3	2	1	0
42. Forgetting important information	3	2	1	0
43. Can't turn off certain thoughts	3	2	1	0

	Nearly Every Day	Every Week	Once or Twice	Never
IX. Eating				
44. Loss of appetite	3	2	1	0
45. Overeating, excessive hunger	3	2	1	0
46. No time to eat	3	2	1	0
X. Activity				
47. Overwhelmed by work	3	2	1	0
48. No time to relax	3	2	1	0
49. Unable to meet commitments or complete tasks	3	2	1	0
XI. Relationships				
50. Withdrawing from relationships	3	2	1	0
51. Feel victimized, taken advantage of	3	2	1	0
52. Loss of sexual interest or pleasure	3	2	1	0
TOTAL I–XI				

A score over 60 indicates significant stress-related distress, although scores can become inflated by the presence of a chronic medical condition. A score above 40 is cause for some concern, and remedial action.

a source of pain and discomfort? Explore your answers to these questions.

Broadly, we can describe sets of negative/unhealthy and positive/healthy attitudes toward your body:

Negative: The body is ignored and its needs or messages are not allowed to enter awareness until serious physical breakdowns or damage have occurred. The body is seen as an enemy, not liked, and not expected to be helpful or come through in a crisis. The body gets sick for no apparent reason.

Write down some of your negative feelings and attitudes toward your body:

_____

_____

_____

_____

Positive: The body is a friend, whom we know well and can count on for help under reasonable circumstances. If we become ill, we know that we have the resources to become well, and we participate in the healing process. We listen to our body, respond to it, and respect its needs. The body is a source of pleasure and positive feelings, which are a meaningful part of our lives. We live in our body as much as we do in our mind, and find that our life is a balance of the two influences, a working partnership.

Write down some of your positive feelings and attitudes toward your body:

_____

_____

_____

_____

Managing stress begins when we make a commitment to develop a positive attitude toward our body. That means using our body to bring us pleasure, and respecting both its wisdom in warning us of difficulty and stress, and its needs. If we pay attention to our bodies, we have gone a long way toward keeping stress from silently slipping into our lives and causing damage. We can spot stress-related difficulty early, and reverse it quickly.

When Stress Builds Up

Think back to the last time you had a headache, or other painful symptom of stress. Were you aware of tension building up earlier, around your scalp and temple?

It is much easier to prevent a headache from occurring in the first place than to get rid of it when it has reached the severe pain level. If we can recognize the early signs, we can take a break—a walk, time out, a short relaxation period—and probably prevent it. Or we can take time before a meal to relax our bodies, to prevent us from eating too fast or too much, due to the tension of our day. We can learn to listen to our bodies, and when we hear signs of tension, use that as a signal to do something to bring us back into balance or change our pace. Too often we react to early signs of stress by telling ourselves that we just have to push harder, as if we are in a race and can beat our headache and finish the job. We think that pushing ourselves makes us more efficient but, in fact, a few short—even three-minute—breaks can give us energy and renewed ability.

Explore what your body is saying to you right now. Check in with your body several times a day. You can become aware of your body's subtle messages—even, one researcher has shown, the firing of one of our billions of nerve cells! Body awareness is a cornerstone of self-care. No physician can know when something is wrong. Many serious ailments are caught in time or are prevented by people who are sensitive to their bodies.

Body awareness is not an invitation to become a complainer. When one is aware of the beginning of a pain, one has a responsibility to do something to change it, not to blame it on others or demand special consideration because of your suffering. Responsible self-care means taking care of your body, not increasing your suffering.

Ineffective Methods of Managing Tension

At the end of a stressful day we all have ways to relax and unwind. Some of them are healthy and pleasurable—a picnic with the family, a game of tennis, or a quiet evening with a person you care for. The day's tension needs to be discharged or else we run the risk of stress-related illnesses—chronic headaches, ulcers, or high blood pressure, for example—developing within our stress-weakened body. By not discharging our daily buildup of tension, we make ourselves vulnerable to all manner of ailments.

Unfortunately, many of the activities listed in Exercise 24 that we commonly use to unwind are not helpful. Some, like an occasional beer or aspirin, are probably not too damaging. Others—smoking, for example—do little to overcome daily tension, but quickly become a habit that undermines our health. The key is balance. Any habit that we use to excess can add to our stress and further harm our health.

TENSION MANAGEMENT ACTIVITIES

People try to deal with stress, strain, pressure, and tension with a variety of habits. Some of these not only do little actually to relieve the pressure, but create additional difficulties or health problems as well.

For the following activities indicate how much of the time during the past month you have utilized them to cope with your daily tension. A total score over 20 indicates difficulty managing tension.

	Every Day	Once or Twice a Week	A Few Times	Never
1. Smoking	3	2	1	0
2. Alcoholic beverages	3	2	1	0
3. Overeating	3	2	1	0
4. Go to sleep	3	2	1	0
5. Television	3	2	1	0
6. Fight with family members	3	2	1	0
7. Angry emotional outbursts	3	2	1	0
8. Tranquilizers	3	2	1	0
9. Aspirin and other pain killers	3	2	1	0
10. Prescription drugs	3	2	1	0
11. Marijuana, cocaine, etc.	3	2	1	0
12. Ignore or deny stress symptoms	3	2	1	0
13. Withdraw from other people	3	2	1	0
14. Criticize, ridicule, or blame other people	3	2	1	0
15. Create conflicted personal or sexual relations				
TOTAL				

METHODS OF RELAXATION

You have been exploring ineffective methods of relieving tension. Now think about the positive things that you do to relax. There is no single effective way to relax. Effective relaxation means that when you are aware of tension building up in your body, you take immediate steps to bring the body back into balance and rest. The tension that builds up may be either physical, mental, or a combination of both.

There are several types of relaxation activities. First, there are rests and diversions. These include short naps, reading a book, seeing a movie, or spending pleasant time with your family. Rests or diversions are very important; people who do not know how to rest and let their mind leave their work or pressures have no outlet to escape or relieve tension.

List your own regular rests and diversions:_____

_____

How often do you use these methods of relaxation, and how effective are they in relieving your daily tensions?_____

_____

A second set of relaxation activities is active physical exercise. People need exercise, otherwise the muscles, including the critically important heart muscle, deteriorate. Regular exercise increases your body's energy and resiliency, and helps create a feeling of well-being. Walking, jogging, riding a bicycle, yoga, or sports like swimming, tennis, racquetball, or golf are all helpful. The method of exercise you select depends on your personal preference. However, some forms of activity, like bicycling or jogging (aerobic exercise), may be more helpful in exercising the heart, and therefore might be indicated if you have high blood pressure or heart disease.

What types of physical activity do you do regularly?_____

_____

A third method of relaxation is passive physical relaxation. This includes massage, acupressure, physical manipulation, and sexual activity. Touching is a basic human need, and some of the tension taking root in the body can be effectively discharged in this way. It also feels good.

What passive physical relaxation methods are a normal part of your life?

Deep Relaxation Techniques

Rest, diversions, and active and passive physical activity alone are not enough to give most people the relaxation they need. Even after rest and strenuous exercise, deep tension can remain in our muscles, and our minds can still be filled with worries and unresolved feelings. We become so accustomed to living with tension that we may not even be consciously aware that deep tension remains with us all the time.

The practice of deep relaxation or meditation is an important part of stress management. Attaining the rest and peace of meditation or deep relaxation seems to be almost a necessity to maintain ourselves, if our lives are full of pressures, change, and demands.

A daily period of deep relaxation helps us in several ways. It discharges deep muscle and physical tensions, and helps us overcome anxiety and attain greater peace of mind. It teaches us to listen and be sensitive to the messages and needs of our bodies. It helps us to achieve greater energy, well-being, and balance.

Cardiologist Herbert Benson of Harvard University, who helped conduct the most important psychological and physiological studies of the effects of meditation and deep relaxation, feels that the body has the capacity to attain a *"relaxation response,"* which is the opposite of the stress response. Both the relaxation and stress responses are necessary to our lives, but each has its place. The stress response equips us for action and sustained high performance. We also have a need for regular periods of relaxation, where tension and stress are released.

Benson notes that the ability to trigger relaxation has been a part of almost every culture in history. They used varieties of meditation, self-hypnosis, and guided mental imagery. Some cultures, like the Hindu and Buddhist religious traditions, evolved highly structured and complex systems for regulating the nervous system, for self-healing, and for calming the body. Our modern reliance on drugs, alcohol, and food to tranquilize ourselves seems to have caused many of us to neglect the development of this natural skill.

Using deep relaxation, meditation, guided imagery, or self-hypnosis, one can shut off the stress response once it has been triggered in a crisis or after a demanding day, or one can train the nervous system to stay calm and not react too drastically to normal stressors. This skill is another cornerstone of self-care: it enables us immediately to reduce the negative effects of stress, relieving many minor physical and emotional stress symptoms.

What Is Relaxation?

Very simply, we can think of the physical state of stress and the state of relaxation as being opposite poles. In the stress state the muscles are tight, the breathing is shallow, the stomach secretes acid, and adrenaline is released throughout the body, which signals "action." When anything triggers the stress response, the body readies itself for action and high performance, whether the threat is physical or psychological.

If direct action is taken against the source of the stress, or if the body is physically activated, the body soon springs back to its normal state. However, if nothing direct or active is done when the stress response is triggered, tension builds in the muscles, and the rest of the body remains in the stressed-out condition. By the end of a day when the stress response has been triggered many times, the result is a state of chronic tension.

Physical activity can release some of the hormonal by-products of the stress response that build up in the body, as can things like massage. But these physical activities often do not affect the other body systems that are pressured. Sleep and rest can also allow the body time to release tension and come back to a normal, balanced state.

Varieties of Deep Relaxation

Americans are attuned to brand names and different varieties, and deep relaxation is no exception. Once we accept our need to learn deep relaxation, we are faced with a host of different methods, each competing for our attention. Are they different from each other? Which one is best?

Research is far from providing answers to these questions. However, it suggests that all the various types of deep relaxation and meditation have more similarities than differences. All techniques help us relax our outer muscles, deepen our breathing, and offer some focus for attention to quiet the mind. They are all done sitting or sometimes lying in a quiet place, with attention focused inward. They all ask us to learn "passive attention"—paying attention to something without forcing, pushing, or aiming at a particular goal or end point.

With those commonalities, each person can choose a method that fits his or her needs and personal style. The authors, and many others, have created cassette relaxation tapes that offer guided imagery or music along with gentle instructions and suggestions. There are transcendental meditation and other forms of meditation, and deep muscle relaxation training and autogenic training, which give suggestions to our body. There is self-hypnosis. And, for those who desire technology to help them, there is biofeedback, offering second-to-second messages on how relaxed our bodies have become to teach us that we are learning to relax. Biofeedback can be used to help us learn any method of relaxation.

Meditation

Another effective tool for relieving stress and tension and building calm and peace into your life is some form of meditation. The meditative experience will provide you with a model of what it feels like to be deeply relaxed. You will discover a mental/physical state of energy, calmness, clarity, and warmth that is both self-empowering and pleasurable. The intention of meditation is to feel that way all of the time.

The basic attitude cultivated in all forms of meditation and relaxation exercises is what is called "passive attention." This is a form of focus of attention that is different from the usual mode of attention during our active life. Ordinarily we are focused on our goals, and we willfully direct our attention at tasks and objects. We often become oblivious to our surroundings, our body, or whatever else that is going on. In meditation or deep relaxation we focus our attention gently, without forcing or concentrating, on some object or process. Our attention is on the immediate process, without any goal or outcome. Paradoxically, the more we *try* to relax or concentrate, just as the harder we try to fall asleep, the more difficult it becomes to achieve the desired state of consciousness. In meditation we focus without forcing or trying. We are open to all of our surroundings, and to the deepest parts of our inner experience.

You can begin to practice relaxing and meditating simply by paying relaxed attention to *anything*—a word, sound, your breath, your body, or some positive feeling state or activity. If your mind wanders, do not force it back to your object, but gently rein it in, back to what you are focusing on. Or alternately, simply allow your mind to go where it wants, observing your own experience, watching but not adding your will to the flow of thoughts, memories, and ideas. As you practice this passive style of attention, you will feel a sense of freedom and peace that comes of letting go or surrendering to the natural, spontaneous, inner process of meditation. It will become a way to contact deeper layers of yourself, an inner reservoir of energy and peace.

You will now learn some of the ways that you can relax or de-stress. The chief thing that you don't do is engage in characteristic thought patterns. In other words, don't think your usual thoughts in your usual way. Surrender them for a brief time—knowing full well that they'll be waiting for you. The intention of meditation and relaxation is to quiet thoughts, to relax them, and to let them go. This is a skill you need to learn, and it takes time and practice. This can be extremely difficult to do. Sometimes it helps to combine strenuous exercise with meditation. Any form of vigorous movement will usually enable you to sit quietly without thinking for a more extended period of time than you're used to.

Some simple self-initiating ways to help quiet your mind include listening to music, following your breath, gazing at a crystal or flower, repeating a tone or sound. They all facilitate a physical state of deep relaxation.

Breath Meditation. This is an easy way to begin your practice of meditation or deep relaxation. This exercise is adopted from simple forms of meditation. It consists of little more than sitting quietly and comfortably, and paying careful attention to your breathing.

Sit in a quiet, secure environment. Close your eyes. Shift your attention from the outside world, and from your cares about your life, to your body and the physical sensations occurring right now. Notice as many sensations in your body as possible.

Pay attention to your breathing. In your mind's eye imagine air going into your lungs as you inhale, going down deep into your abdomen, and then imagine the air going out as you exhale. For a few minutes, just experience your breathing. If your mind wanders or you fall asleep, when you become aware of this, bring your mind back to your breathing.

As you inhale (through your nose if that is comfortable), count to yourself, "one." As you exhale, through your mouth, say "and." For the next breath continue your count—"two, and." When you get to four, begin again with "one, and." If you lose the count, start with "one."

Continue for ten to twenty minutes, or as long as you feel comfortable doing the exercise. Slowly open your eyes, and sit for a minute.

You can also meditate by selecting an object that attracts your attention. Sit quietly, spine erect, for ten to twenty minutes, gazing at the object. Give it your undivided attention. If say, a flower is before you, feel, taste, and sense its shape, color, and fragrance. Become the flower—dissolve into it. If distracting thoughts pass through your mind, accept them and let them go. Then gently go back to the object of your attention, without pushing yourself. It will take a while to get used to this. After a session you will feel relaxed, refreshed, and rejuvenated.

Guidelines for Deep Relaxation

The following pages offer directions for several types of simple relaxation and meditation exercises. You should make a commitment to practice them daily for a period of several weeks so that you can accurately assess their effects on your stress level and well-being.

Here are some general instructions for how to begin the regular practice of relaxation.

Daily practice: Relaxation is a form of physical training. It has no effect unless it is done regularly. Also, like any form of physical training, such as a sport, you have to learn how to do it. It is not a magic health cure for stress; it is a way of training your body to enter a deep, regenerative state. Some people can learn it quickly; others will take time, or need to work individually with an instructor.

For your initial practice allow enough time to learn something about relaxation. Do not attempt to assess its effects, or your own performance, until you have practiced it for two weeks. The effects may not be apparent until then. You may have trouble for the first day or two, such as finding it difficult to concentrate, or feeling some momentary increase in stress level of discomfort. Continue practicing, unless you develop some serious difficulty (this is rare).

Develop a routine: Habits can be good or bad. If you make a regular time and place to do your deep relaxation, you will be creating a habit that you soon will look forward to, and do automatically.

To help you develop a routine, and to help you keep a record of your progress and difficulties, use a relaxation log, which you can fill out briefly before and after each of your relaxation periods. Keeping a chart for the first several weeks is a useful incentive and allows you to see graphically that you are making progress, lest you forget. Also, if you are learning in a class or from an instructor, you have a record to bring to class, so that you can discuss difficulties and problems.

An important part of developing a routine is to create a safe, protected place to relax. That means asking for help from the people around you, leaving your phone off the hook, and doing whatever is necessary to ensure that you will not be disturbed. Create a special place, or part of a room, to do your exercise.

Time and posture: The best time to do a relaxation exercise is before a meal. Many people relax early in the morning, and just before dinner. It can also be done after or during a stressful activity.

The usual posture for deep relaxation is sitting straight in a chair, hands folded in your lap, feet flat on the floor. If you need back support, place a pillow behind you. You can also use a recliner chair, or even lie down, although these postures make it more likely you will fall asleep during the exercise.

Mental attitude: The mental attitude required for deep relaxation is opposite the mind-set required for most task-oriented activities. Sometimes it takes a while to become comfortable with the attitude of "passive attention" (or passive volition). Do not push yourself, or try too hard to concentrate. Rather let your attention focus on what you have decided to focus on—your breath, your muscles, a mental picture. If your mind wanders, and it surely will many times in the course of each exercise, simply finish the thought and then bring your mind back to your object of attention. Do not be critical of yourself, or try to keep your mind from wandering. This will only defeat you and make you tense up while you are trying to relax. Many people wrongly expect that their minds will be blank during their exercises. This state of mind comes only after years of guided instruction and daily practice. Do not frustrate yourself with unrealistic expectations.

Passive attention has been described as paying attention to the

(text continues on page 173)

EXERCISE 25

ACTIVITIES THAT PROMOTE RELAXATION

In column A indicate how many times per week you engage in each activity. In column B indicate how frequently you would like to engage in each activity.

Active Relaxation Activities

	A	B		A	B
Sports	___	___	Jogging	___	___
Dancing	___	___	Stretching	___	___
Laughing	___	___	Yoga	___	___
Walking	___	___	Sex	___	___
			Other _____	___	___

Deep Relaxation Activities

	A	B		A	B
Massage	___	___	Deep muscle relaxation	___	___
Hypnosis	___	___	Progressive relaxation	___	___
Self-hypnosis	___	___	Mantras or sound focus	___	___
Autogenics	___	___	Breath focus	___	___
Biofeedback	___	___	Mandalas or visual focus	___	___
Guided imagery	___	___	Instant relaxation	___	___
			Other meditation _____	___	___

RELAXATION LOG

Before you start your relaxation, note in column 1 the stressful events in your day preceding your relaxation. In column 2 write down your prerelaxation S/R (stress/relaxation) level, using a subjective scale of 1–10 (1 reflects total relaxation, while 10 indicates being very highly stressed or tense). Put it after "before."

Do your relaxation exercise.

After the exercise, note your stress or relaxation level again, in the appropriate "after" location, using the 1–10 scale.

Then fill in some of the thoughts, feelings, body experiences, and/or other distinguishing occurrences during your relaxation period in column 3.

For week of: _____

A.M. RELAXATION

Stressful Events of the Morning	S/R Levels 1–10	Experiences during relaxation: feelings, thoughts, etc.
MONDAY	Before ____ After ____	
TUESDAY	Before ____ After ____	
WEDNESDAY	Before ____ After ____	
THURSDAY	Before ____ After ____	
FRIDAY	Before ____ After ____	
SATURDAY	Before ____ After ____	
SUNDAY	Before ____ After ____	

P.M. RELAXATION

Stressful Events of the Evening	S/R Levels 1–10	Experiences during relaxation: feelings, thoughts, etc.
	Before ____ After ____	
	Before ____ After ____	
	Before ____ After ____	
	Before ____ After ____	
	Before ____ After ____	
	Before ____ After ____	
	Before ____ After ____	

process, rather than to the goal. Do not think about getting relaxed, which is your goal; pay attention to whatever sensation you are having at the moment, no matter what it is. If you find it hard to do the exercise, or to relax, pay attention to your body and try to find out why. You may need to do something, write something down, make a phone call, or finish a task before you are fully ready to relax.

Problems and discomfort: Because we all have expectations about the benefits of relaxation, many people begin to practice a relaxation exercise and feel they are not doing it right. It seems too simple! Their experience does not fit their expectations, however vague and unrealistic these expectations may be. In fact almost everyone is doing the exercise correctly. Trust yourself.

Sometimes a person will experience some discomfort, either physical tension or anxiety, during or after a deep relaxation exercise. This is because in relaxing you may become aware of tension in your body that you had ignored or not even realized, or you may be letting feelings or thoughts into conscious awareness that you had previously repressed. In most cases the antidote is to wait for a while and then continue the exercise. However, if discomfort or anxiety persists, it is wise to work with an instructor until these reactions can be halted.

Deep Muscle Relaxation

Many people are not sensitive to the degree of tension that builds up in their muscles during a day of even quiet work. This exercise is designed to help you become aware of the difference between tension and relaxation in each of the major muscle groups. This exercise also incorporates some of the suggestions that are part of autogenic training (e.g., heaviness and warmth in the arms, coolness in the forehead), which help to create the deep relaxation state.

1. Sit or lie comfortably, and close your eyes. Become aware of how tense or relaxed your body is, and pay attention to your body for a few moments.

2. Make a fist and tense your right hand (if you are right-handed) for a few seconds, then relax and let it go loose. Then, tell your hands to become warm and heavy, and help the suggestion by imagining things like a heavy weight tied to your hand, or the sun beating down on it.

3. Next tense and relax your right forearm, and then follow it up with suggestions and images for it to become heavy and warm. Then do the same with the upper arm, shoulder, and then the right foot, lower leg, and upper leg. Your whole right side should feel relaxed, heavy, and warm.

4. Repeat the procedure with the left side (or other side). Your hands, arms, feet, and legs should now be relaxed, heavy, and warm. Wait for these feelings, or repeat the procedure again. It may take a few repetitions before you can do this. When you have mastered heaviness and warmth, you may be able to relax the muscles without having to tense them first.

5. Now relax the muscles of the hips, and imagine that a wave of relaxation is passing up from the abdomen to the chest. Imagine the wave coming in as you inhale, bringing deep relaxation, and then imagine the wave receding as you exhale. Do not tense these muscles. Tell the hips, the abdomen, and the chest to become heavy and warm. Let each breath become deeper, completely filling the abdomen. Wait for your breathing to become very deep before going on to the next stage of the exercise.

6. Next, imagine as you inhale that a wave of relaxation is continuing into the shoulders, to the neck, the jaw, the mouth, up to the face, and to the scalp. Relax each muscle group in turn, imagining the relaxation passing over it. Pay special attention to the muscles controlling the eyes and forehead. (If you wear contact lenses, you should remove them before doing this exercise.) Now suggest to your brow to be cool, and imagine a breeze or a cold compress touching your forehead.

7. Enjoy the feeling of deep relaxation. In your mind's eye imagine that you are in a lovely, peaceful, relaxing spot, without a care in the world. Imagine the scene with all of your senses—feeling, hearing, smelling, seeing, and even tasting what it is like to be in that special place.

8. When you are ready to finish the exercise, take two deep breaths, and then open your eyes. Sit quietly for a moment or two.

Breath Awareness

Sit in a balanced position. Settle into your chair so you feel as little strain as possible on your lower back or abdominal muscles. Imagine a cord attached to the top of your head, pulling your spine perfectly straight and aligned from the top of your head to the bottom of your spine. Move your feet around until they are both comfortably placed on the floor, approximately one and a half feet apart and with your calves perpendicular to the floor. Lift your hands and drop them to your thighs. Now visualize the cord being cut and allow your head to move very slowly to a comfortable position.

Take a deep breath and gently and easily exhale.

Allow your next breath to be the one your body takes itself, and watch your abdomen expand as you breathe in and contract as you breathe out.

When you feel settled into your breathing, say to yourself on each in breath, "I am . . ." and on each out breath ". . . relaxed": "I am relaxed." Allow your body to slip into relaxation easily and comfortably.

Continue this practice and soon you will be able to relax simply by taking a deep breath.

Muscle Relaxation with Guided Imagery

This exercise can be done either sitting up or lying down. You might read the instructions onto a cassette tape, slowly, and then play them back to yourself as you follow the suggestion.

Begin this process with the "breath awareness" exercise.

Slightly tense your hands, arms, and shoulders. Concentrate on the tension and how it feels. Now very slowly begin to relax down through your shoulders, arms and forearms. Be aware of how it feels as you release the tension and replace it with relaxation. Relax your wrists, hands, and fingers, and now imagine this feeling of relaxation flowing downward through your body, all the way down to your toes. Pause.

Gently contract and tense your scalp, forehead, eyelids, tissue around your eyes, your mouth and jaw muscles. Be aware of the tension. Slowly begin to relax your scalp, forehead, eyelids, tissues around your eyes. Be aware of how it feels as you release the tension and replace it with relaxation. Relax your mouth muscles and jaw muscles. Now, using your creative imagination, imagine this feeling of relaxation flowing on down through your neck, shoulders, arms, and hands. Imagine this sense of relaxation going through your chest and abdominal area, on down through your hips, legs, calves, and feet, all the way to the tips of your toes. Pause.

Take a deep breath and tighten the muscles in your chest and abdomen and then while exhaling, allow your chest and abdomen to relax completely. Imagine relaxing your chest and abdominal area internally. Imagine all the organs, glands, even the cells, functioning in a relaxed, normal, healthy manner. Now tighten your hips, legs, feet, and toes. Slowly begin to release the tension down through your hips, legs, calves, ankles, feet, and toes. Pause.

Imagine that you have plugs in your big toes and that any tension remaining in your body is like water. Imagine that you have pulled these plugs and the tension begins to drain out of your toes. As it does, again imagine a deep sense of relaxation flowing from the scalp down through the forehead, eyelids, face, and jaw muscles. Imagine this feeling of relaxation flowing down through your neck, shoulders, arms, and hands. Allow this feeling of relaxation to flow on downward throughout your chest and abdominal area, through your hips and legs, all the way down to the tips of your toes. Take a moment to imagine a state of mental and physical well-being and complete relaxation.

Give yourself ample time to come out of this state of relaxation. Before opening your eyes, and as you open them, flex your arms by bending them at the elbows and stretch them above your head several times.

Gentle Muscle Relaxation

Note: Because of the subtleness of this exercise, work only on one side of your body, preferably your dominant side.

Begin with the "breath awareness" exercise.

Throughout this exercise attend to your breathing and any other parts of your body that might be tensing unnecessarily. Pay special attention to your shoulders, jaw muscles, and your eyes. As you perform this exercise, tense only to the point where you notice the tension.

Bend the toes of your right foot under slightly. Hold on to this slight pressure while you examine your breathing and the rest of your body. When you let go, feel the entire right side of your body relax.

Lift your toes off the ground. Hold on to this pressure while you mentally examine your jaw muscles, your shoulder muscles, your eyes, and your breathing. Very gently, allow your toes to come back to the floor and feel the entire right side of your body relax.

Push your heel down on the ground with just enough pressure to feel some slight tensing of your muscles. Repeat your check of body muscles and breathing. Very slowly, allow that tension in your calf muscles to go away. You will feel your right side relax even more.

Lift your heel off the ground and feel your thigh muscles slightly contract. Hold on to that tension while you mentally examine the rest of your body. Especially check your breath, keeping it calm and regular. See that you haven't clenched your teeth, and that your eyes are relaxed. Carefully allow your heel to come back to the floor and enter relaxation once again.

Pick your right hand up and bend your wrist toward your elbow until you feel your forearm tighten. Hold it while you check your shoulders and breathing, your jaw muscles and eyes, and then gradually let it go, and feel your arm suffused with new energy and relaxation.

Bend your arm at the elbow to slightly tense your biceps muscles. Don't do a powerful demonstration, just enough to feel that slight muscular tension. This time pay special attention to your shoulders, and also check to see that you haven't tightened up your right hand in the process. Check your breathing, your jaw muscles, and your eyes. Then let it all go, easily and gently.

Push your right hand down onto your right thigh, until you feel your triceps muscle tighten. Your shoulder will rise slightly, but your jaw and eyes shouldn't tense. Continue to breathe calmly and regularly. Hold on to that tension while the rest of you remains relaxed, and then let go of that tension.

One final movement: lift your right hand and right leg and make small circles. Continue to breathe, and then let it all go.

Get up and walk around the room, paying attention to the differences between your right and left sides.

Reeducating Your Stress Response

This practice will teach you to relax yourself deeply. It is a two-part exercise that will first help you to become increasingly aware of the physical tension you are carrying and then introduce you to a superb tool for instantly reducing stress—guided imagery.

Make sure that you will not be interrupted for several minutes. Sit or lie in any comfortable position. Most people are able to sit relaxed for a period of time when their spines are relatively straight. Back and neck support are helpful with feet flat on the floor, and hands on the arm of the chair or in your lap. The exercise can also be done while lying down, but you run the risk of falling asleep.

Sit quietly for a few moments. Close your eyes gently. Become aware of all the sense impressions and feelings that arise from your body when you shift your awareness from the outside world to your inner world. Simply sit patiently and pay attention to your body. Hear what it says to you. You will be able to shift your awareness to different bodily parts and discover feelings that are ordinarily unconscious. Explore these bodily messages; they are important. They teach you the effects your life has on your body.

Let the following suggestions take root within you. If your mind wanders, or you fall asleep for a few moments, simply refocus and continue. Self-criticism and blame will only get in your way.

Take a long, deep breath, filling your chest, and allow the breath to flow deep into your abdomen. Hold your breath for a second or two, and then exhale. You will feel an immediate relaxation and increasing awareness as you breathe fully and deeply. Follow your breath for a few moments, and see how this affects your body. Are you more relaxed? What changes have taken place?

Focus your attention on your arms and hands. Become aware of them. Explore the muscles in your arms, hands, and fingers and see if there is any tension in them. If you discover tension, take a deep breath and imagine that your breath is moving from your lungs directly through your arms and hands, bringing with it a feeling of warmth and relaxation. Exhale, and imagine that the muscle tension from your hands and arms is flowing out with each breath, leaving your hands and arms deeply relaxed.

Focus on head, neck, shoulders, chest, abdomen, back and spine, hips, buttocks, and legs in the same manner. Remember to give relaxation suggestions for each part in turn.

Enjoy this relaxed state and the peaceful feelings that go along with it. Let each breath carry you deeper and deeper into the relaxation state.

Imagine seeing, feeling, hearing, smelling, and tasting a place of beauty and peace where you feel completely relaxed. It may be somewhere that you once visited, or a place that exists only in your imagination. Create this special environment for yourself as vividly as you can. What does it feel like, what do you see, hear, smell, taste? Do something with each of your senses. Relax and enjoy your special place.

Now imagine that while you are there you are in a state of perfect, optimal health and well-being. What are you doing? How do you feel? What do you look like? Enjoy the experience.

Slowly bring your attention back to the room, keeping with you the feeling of peace, relaxation, and well-being. You can return to your personal relaxation and healing place whenever you wish. We recommend that you do so at least once a day.

Stretching and Body Relaxation

Sit in a comfortable position. Allow your hands to hang down by your sides, and take in a full breath of air and exhale easily.

On your next inhalation bring your head and torso easily erect, and as you exhale, allow your head to fall gently forward. Continue breathing, directing your breath into the back of your neck. Inhale and bring your head to an erect position. As you exhale, slowly allow your head to fall backward. If you allow your mouth to open, your head can relax even more. Continue breathing, feeling any fullness or tightness in your neck. Breathe in, and allow your head once again to come erect. Breathe easily and feel the degree of relaxation that is obtained from even this simple motion if done with awareness.

Take another breath of air, and allow your right ear to fall toward your right shoulder. Exhale and breathe into the area that is stretching on the left side of your neck. Feel the tension in any of the muscles of your shoulders and neck. Slowly lift your right shoulder up toward your right ear. They may touch, but it isn't necessary that they do. Keep the motion easy and comfortable as your ear and shoulder come together. Hold this position for a moment. When you feel ready, allow your shoulder to descend *slowly*, so you can experience your muscles letting go. You might feel some jerking in this motion. You may also notice that once you reach the area where your shoulder was when you began, you can release it now so that it drops even lower.

Slowly take another breath and allow your head to come erect. Breathe easily and feel the difference between your left and right shoulders.

Repeat on the left side.

Because most people experience their greatest amount of tension in the region of their shoulders and neck, do some neck rolls. Never jerk or force the neck. Always allow it to move much as if it were on ball bearings, easily going in a circle.

Begin by allowing your head to fall backward as you inhale. Slowly begin turning your head toward the left. As your head moves toward the front, begin exhaling, slowly and carefully watching your head move in this position. As your head begins to turn toward the right, begin to inhale toward the back position. Repeat this, inhaling as your head is in the rear position and exhaling as your head is toward the front. When you have completed two neck rolls in a clockwise direction, reverse the direction and do two neck rolls counterclockwise. Inhale and bring your head easily erect. Sit comfortably and feel your neck and shoulders.

Bring your arms in close to the sides of your body, and begin also to raise your shoulders at the same time, as if you were trying to touch both shoulders to your ears. As you slowly exhale, allow your shoulders to come down. As they reach their lowest position, breathe easily and shake your hands just a little bit, and gently move your shoulders.

Place your hands in the small of your back so that your thumbs are pointing toward your abdomen. Take a breath and lean backward, or arch your back a little bit to feel some tension in your abdomen. As you exhale, allow your torso to come forward. As you inhale, let your breath help to straighten you up. Repeat.

Allow your hands to position themselves on your hips. Breathe easily, and as you exhale, stretch to the right. Inhale and come erect. Exhale and lean to the left. Repeat.

Raise your right leg, place your hands around your knee and leg, and pull your whole leg into your chest so you can feel some pulling on your lower back. Hold on to it for a moment, breathing into your lower back, and then allow your right leg to return to the floor. Repeat on the left side, just pulling to that area where you feel stretching but are still comfortable.

Close your eyes and sit quietly, listening to the sounds of your body. Hear and feel the silence within.

Notice a full flow of breath of air at your nostrils. Watch the change of direction as you breathe out. On each inhalation say to yourself, "I am . . ." and on each exhalation, ". . . relaxed." In and out as you move into a deeper and deeper state of alert relaxation. Pause. Discontinue all breathing exercises and simply watch the fullness of your breath, the continuous flow. Experience the silence between the in and out breaths.

Slowly begin to move your toes, your feet, your legs. Rock back and forth in your chair, move your shoulders, arms, and hands. Easily turn your head and when you feel ready, take a full breath of air, and open your eyes, feeling relaxed, rejuvenated, and comfortable.

Quick Relaxation Techniques

There are a wealth of things that we can do when we are under stress. Some of the techniques suggested below are time-honored, and we have all used them. Others are new and we need to experiment with them and see how they work for us. Any of these techniques will work, provided we tune in to our need early enough, and immediately take action.

Here is a list of quick relaxation techniques. You can add to the list.

1. Take a five-minute break. Take a walk, sit or lie quietly, have a chat with someone.

2. Take a short nap.

3. Spend a few moments imagining a peaceful, relaxing scene or event in your life. Recall it in detail, imagining what it felt like with all your senses. Or imagine something pleasant that you are looking forward to doing in the near future, or something that you might do to reward yourself when the pressure or task is over.

4. Massage your forehead, your eyes, or the back of your neck. You might learn some acupressure first-aid techniques.

5. Deep breathing. Take a deep breath, let it go deeply into your abdomen. Hold it for a few seconds and slowly exhale. This automatically sends a message to the body to relax.

6. Do any deep relaxation technique for a few moments. Imagine your muscles relaxing.

7. Run outside, or yell or scream for a few minutes if you can do it safely. Stretch your muscles actively to release tension.

8. Switch to another job for a change of pace.

CHAPTER 8

Peak Performance and Creativity

Most cultures accord the highest honors, respect, and admiration to those people who demonstrate the highest level of skill—in athletics, in the arts, for invention, and for political leadership. We honor not simply the beauty or worth of what they have done, but also the dedication, energy commitment, and single-mindedness of their paths toward their goals. They represent the highest ideals of achievement of the things that we value most.

If the burned-out or impaired individual represents the low end of the scale, the high end is represented by these peak performers. To a degree, peak performance reflects special ability. However, we can learn how to do things better. This is true not only in such areas as sports, but in everyday life as well.

Peak performers are not always obvious superstars. In every workplace there are people who are obviously stressed and burned out and there are obvious leaders and high achievers. But there are also people who, surprisingly and even somewhat invisibly, keep increasing their level of performance. They may become deeply involved in a particular project or area, and deliver unexpectedly creative work. How do we account for people suddenly overreaching themselves?

Much of what has been learned comes from the study of people who are peak performers. Psychologist Abraham Maslow suggested twenty years ago that psychology spends too much time studying sick people. It should turn its attention to not just ordinary healthy people, but the special minority who demonstrated the highest levels of health and achievement. Just as we have learned from people who exemplify wellness and ability to manage stress, so we have begun to learn from the people who consistently deliver peak levels of performance.

Psychologist Charles Garfield has studied more than a thousand

peak performers—athletes, astronauts, survivors of life-threatening illness, managers, leaders, writers, and performers—and from their reports he has distilled some of their common skills, attitudes, and
qualities. What is most interesting is how many of these common elements exist no matter what the nature of the performance—whether
physical, creative, or interpersonal.

The study of peak performers leads us to the end of our exploration of burnout. Overcoming burnout is more than simply coping well
and managing oneself and situations. There is a way in which avoiding
burnout is a creative act. Staying in one place, doing things the same
way, even if they work, can over time become a source of de-energiz-
ing stress. People need to grow, expand, and be creative. As George
Land put it, the choice for people is to "grow or die." The person who
successfully manages stress and avoids burnout moves toward peak
performance.

Health and well-being are not incompatible with creativity and
achievement. Studies of peak performers cast doubt on such myths as
the maladjusted or alienated artist, the lonely and isolated leader, the
solitary athlete, or the person who succeeds at great cost to himself
and those around him. In fact, peak performers are commonly found
to be healthy, social, satisfied, and fulfilled.

The factors that enhance peak performance are those that promote
health, well-being, and self-esteem. The theme of this book is that
self-management and self-renewal are not simply ways to keep oneself
from self-destructing; they are pathways toward optimal performance
and creative living.

This chapter begins by noting the skills, attitudes, and qualities
that characterize peak performers. Next we see the role of belief systems to limit or expand one's capacities, and the role of creative and
intuitive thought styles to lead us in new directions. When people are
fully functioning, they enter the "flow state"—a state of mind that is
different from both ordinary reality and the relaxation state. Some
exercises are presented for moving into the flow state, and then some
of the ways we can move toward our own peak performances. Finally,
the chapter, and the book, ends with a discussion of the commonalities
and links between creative individual performances and creative organizations.

THE PEAK PERFORMER

Garfield's research on the qualities of peak performers and their
personal styles echoes the work of Suzanne Kobasa, Abraham Maslow,
and others who have looked at health and full human functioning. The
authors have distilled the findings of these studies into three basic
orientations: peak performers are inner-directed, pro-active, and self-
caring.

Inner-Directed

Peak performers are aware of and attuned to their inner processes. They are more sensitive to the inner experience of the task than to how the performance will be viewed or evaluated by others. Peak performers satisfy themselves; they reach goals that they have set for themselves. They feel that they are doing what they want to do.

In addition the goals of the peak performer are clear, concrete, and self-generated. They are not unrealistic or abstract; they are goals that the peak performer visualizes clearly and literally sees himself or herself reaching. Peak performers commit time, energy, and disciplined action to reaching a goal. The beliefs and expectations of peak performers are that they can do things that they have not done before —each day they can do more, differently or better.

Peak performers are by definition people who are in a continual process of self-discovery, reaching within themselves to discover new potentials and new capacities. They accomplish this through a deep inner sense of purpose about what they are doing. They have a sense of *mission,* which carries them sometimes beyond their own expectations. They have the capacity to surprise themselves.

Their internal thought processes are different from other people's. Many of us experience our beliefs as a set of clear limits—what we cannot do, what our organization will not permit, the way things are done, our own personality and skill levels. When we see these things as fixed and limiting, then we can never exceed our previous accomplishments. Peak performers see everything as something to be questioned, tested, and transcended. Peak performers, as management theorist Rosabeth Moss Kanter puts it, are "change masters." They are always looking for new ways to do things and for oblique solutions to persistent problems.

Pro-Active

The peak performer is never satisfied with what he has done the day before. What he can already do well is a source of satisfaction, but his focus is on what he can learn to do next. In all areas the peak performer does not remain in the "comfort zone"; he is continually transcending past performances, exploring new capacities, experiences, and skills. The peak performer is willing to take a chance and do something less well at first.

The peak performer has very little fear of failure. Any new and creative effort is a success. He knows that risk and innovation demand that sometimes one fails. But failure can be a learning experience, not necessarily an assault on self-esteem or a permanent status. A mistake or failure is a valuable teacher, and the capacity to learn from mistakes is a hallmark of the pathway toward peak performance.

In the first stages of any new task a person inevitably suffers a diminished capacity and capability. For example, before beginning to write this book, the authors bought a word processor. Initially our ability to work suffered, as we had to learn a whole new way of thinking and working. But we wanted to enhance our long-term ability to write and consult. After a break-in period, our ability to do our work has expanded. However, developing our skill demanded the willingness to tolerate an initial period of decline.

The peak performer has a bias for action. He is not burdened by perfectionism or inhibition. Instead of attempting, often unrealistically, to achieve a high level of performance at tasks that are less important, or that demand quick responses, the peak performer is able to do the best he can, not the best that would be possible with infinite time and resources. Of course, with major tasks or goals the peak performer is not satisfied with a second-rate effort. While this may seem contradictory, in fact, peak performers are able to walk a tightrope— doing their best and striving for excellence on priority tasks, while knowing that perfect performance is not needed for lesser priorities. And, most important, they are clear which tasks belong in which category.

How does a peak performer keep things straight? The answer is that he is an instinctive planner. While peak performers seem just to know what to do, or just to dive into a project, they are in fact always working out of a flexible but clear inner plan to attain their goals.

While some forms of peak performance are solitary efforts, that is the exception. Most performances depend on concerted efforts of several people. In an organization the peak performer is easily spotted. He does not get bogged down in details; he is a visionary who is able to articulate clearly a sense of purpose and the reasons behind it, and to inspire others to work on the project. People feel invited in, not coerced or manipulated, and they tend to enjoy their participation. Peak performance, like burnout, tends to be contagious.

Another quality of the peak performer, is that when working with others he is less interested in blaming someone else for failures or problems than with finding out how to solve the problem. Similarly, he does not blame himself, or spend time brooding over his own responsibility. He simply does what he can do at the time to correct or complete tasks.

Self-Caring

In this category, once again the reality of peak performers and the mythology diverge. Popular myth has it that effective work is synonymous with overwork, and that the peak performer is a one-sided, workaholic, hard-driving, Type A machine. Not true. The peak performer, attuned to her inner needs and goals, is a model of balance. Peak performers work hard, but they also know how to stop and play. Since the peak performer, in contrast to some (not all) workaholics and

Type A individuals, is a good time manager and works well with others, she does not have to dedicate every waking moment to the pursuit of her goals.

The peak performer knows that her self—including psyche and body—is her vehicle and tool for living; her inner awareness leads her to take good care of herself. The peak performer knows how to relax. Indeed creative thought and planning have been linked to relaxed states. The awareness that fulfilling personal relationships and time with family and friends are enriching and refueling, is deeply ingrained in the peak performer.

The defining element of the peak performer is a sense of *balance*. She is able to balance competing goals and demands, competing skills and needs of other people, and her own varied needs, goals, and abilities. The honing of the ability to excel in a specific area demands a general enhancement of one's self in many areas. One-sidedness is limiting, not an aspect of high effectiveness. Very few tasks demand only one kind of skill, or one person.

Your Own Peak Performances

All of us have had times when we achieved our peak performance —a task, a contest, a job—when we really felt that we were transcending our limits. Think back on your own peak performances. For every peak performance that you can remember, ask yourself these questions:

1. What made me select this task or goal?
2. How did I decide to mobilize the required energy?
3. What resources did I draw on?
4. What was my state of mind during the task?
5. How did I break down the task and go about my work?
6. What were the most essential, critical factors to my achievement?
7. How did my final achievement compare to my expectations, and to my previous abilities and limits?

This exploration of your achievements will yield a list of elements that help you to promote your peak performance. Think about your current work and life situations. How could you incorporate some of these elements?

THE FLOW STATE

Almost every type of peak performance takes place when the performer is in a particular state of mind. This mode of awareness is different from both ordinary awareness and the relaxation state. In effect it combines qualities from ordinary active awareness and relaxation. The hybrid state of mind that is experienced by peak performers is, curiously, the same state of mind that is encountered when one is absorbed in play.

Psychologist Mihaly Czikszentmihalyi has spent many years studying the special state of mind that is characterized by play and by peak performances. He calls it the "flow state."

> Flow denotes the wholistic sensation present when we act with total involvement. It is the kind of feeling after which one nostalgically says "that was fun," or "that was enjoyable." It is the state in which action follows upon action according to an internal logic which seems to need no conscious intervention on our part. We experience it as a unified flowing from one moment to the next, in which we feel in control of our actions, and in which there is little distinction between self and environment; between stimulus and response; or between past, present and future.

He notes that the flow state is associated not just with play, but with creativity, meaningful work, games, athletics, and collective religious rituals. Generally, the activity that one does in this state is done well, close to one's capacity, and with pleasure and deep involvement. Czikszentmihalyi also notes that the flow state is produced when the activity is right at the limit of one's capabilities. If the task is below one's capacity, it is boring and one lacks involvement; if it is too far above, then one gets anxious, and the flow is lost. Therefore, entering the flow state takes place when one is expanding the borders of one's capacity by taking risks.

The flow state has many commonalities with relaxation because in both states one is deeply involved and feels a merging of self with action. The differences lie in the fact that the flow state is a state of concentrated, integrated action. While one may have a relaxed state of mind, physically one is poised for action and involved in the external task at hand.

The most important quality of the flow state is that we are deeply absorbed in the immediate process of what we are doing, not what the outcome, product, or result will be. We are involved in the process of doing the task right now.

Entering the Flow State

Entering the flow state is a prerequisite for peak performance. In many tasks that occurs naturally, and each of us should be deeply familiar with the flow state. The difficulty is in bringing it about purposely.

The following exercise cultivates the flow state by tapping into our psychophysical memory of our various past peak performances.

Stand with your feet comfortably apart, your arms at your sides, and your eyes closed. Shake out your muscles gently until you feel a pleasant warmth or tingling. Take a few deep breaths, feeling the air filling up your lungs and then going down to your abdomen. You should be relaxed, yet able to move.

Let your mind go back to a time when you were in the flow state —it may be an athletic performance, a game, or a work task where you felt completely absorbed and working near to your capacity. Visualize that event in detail, remembering the pleasant absorption and feeling of satisfaction as you accomplished it. Let your body recall the feelings. Enjoy it.

Now think of another type of activity where you entered the flow state, and go through the recollection again. Let your body feel the sensations of being in the flow state. You can let yourself move around, sway, or whatever.

When the feeling of the flow state is deeply within you, begin to visualize a task that you have facing you. This should be a task that you would like to dedicate yourself to achieving at your highest capacity. Think about what it will be like to do that task, with your body and psyche keeping the feelings of the flow state. See yourself remaining in this pleasant, involved, satisfying state as you immerse yourself deeply in the chosen task. See yourself doing the task well, and see yourself feeling good about it. When you complete the task, look at what you have done, and allow yourself to be deeply affected by the feelings that the completion arouses within you.

By doing this exercise when you approach a task, you begin to associate the new task with previous experiences of the flow state. You suggest to your body to enter that state and you block the entry into states of frustration, obsessive concern, anxiety, boredom, or disconnection.

BELIEFS AND VISIONS

Charles Garfield notes that the peak performers he interviewed routinely saw themselves in concrete, detailed, visual imagery, accomplishing and practicing their peak performances. In contrast, people who exaggerate or amplify their stress levels see themselves in their minds as continually failing, or visualize all the bad things that might happen. An essential component of all peak performances is mental preparation. It is as if the mind is a delicate, high-performance computer, and the process of programming and preparing it to transcend its own limits is to set a new model or template for action through imagination.

Therefore, an essential part of preparation for peak performance and effective action involves the mental rehearsal of the activity. In the morning before you tackle a task, or even in the few moments before you start, cultivate a positive image of what you would like to accomplish. See yourself doing it, and tell yourself that you can achieve it. Give yourself suggestions that you can do it well, and compliment yourself in advance for doing it.

The greatest obstacle to peak performance and personal effectiveness has nothing to do with lack of ability. We have all sorts of names and labels for what stops us—lack of desire, not sticking to things, no time, a sense that we can't do something, other people get in our way. These reasons are all rationalizations for not doing something. Telling ourselves that we do not believe that we can do things or we do not believe that we can change things in the future becomes its own truth.

Beliefs are not concrete structures, walls that prevent things from happening. They are structures that guide our lives and determine our actions. Peak performers are capable of envisioning themselves as changing and growing; they do not accept limiting beliefs about themselves and their environments.

List some of your beliefs about your limits. List your reasons for these beliefs, or the experiences that you base them on. Some beliefs are based on past negative experiences. These are real experiences, but they should not be the basis for the conclusion that everything will remain that way. In some cases self-limiting beliefs are based on erroneous conclusions about real experiences, and in other cases they are simply untested assumptions.

From your list of limiting beliefs, examine how each one is an obstacle to your transcendence and accomplishment. For each one think of an experiment that could disprove that belief. Next write a statement that is the opposite of the belief. Say the new statement to yourself a few times, and imagine what would happen if it were true. For example, a limiting belief might be that nobody at work is helpful. You may indeed have experienced people being unhelpful to you and, on reflection, you might remember an equal number of instances when people were helpful. You might also see that sometimes people weren't helpful because you didn't ask for help. Thus the belief becomes something that you can change by testing it. You could say to yourself, "I can expect to get help from my colleagues sometimes," and could actually see yourself doing that.

GOALS AND IDEALS

Peak performance involves a shift in the way we perceive our past, present, and future. Our past beliefs, accomplishments, failures, and constraints are our collective experience. The past is a resource and a repository of learning, not a limit. The present is the point at which we live; it consists of many possibilities for action and the process of choosing. The future is not the same as the past. It is a theater of possibilities and potentials. We can only dimly sense what we are capable of and what we can achieve. So how do we move toward our future? What guides us are our personal goals and our visions of ideals.

The second type of obstacle to achieving peak performance has to do with why we are seeking achievement. Many times we find ourselves not doing something, not completing a task, or not doing well, and we get frustrated. However, a more helpful attitude is to ask ourselves what we can learn from the fact that we are not engaged in the task. Often we discover conflict about why we want to do that task. Sometimes the goal is somebody else's. This doesn't mean that it can never be our goal, but before it can, we need to go through the process of choosing it for ourselves.

Peak performances and creative achievements are characterized by a deep, concentrated focus. The person has to *want* to do something. This mission comes from several sources—it feels good, there are rewards (internal and external), or the goal is shared by important people or society as a whole. There is often a linking of the individual task with some higher purpose or sense of meaning, which sustains the added energy.

When we are blocked because we have not freely or fully chosen something as our goal, we need to ask what the task offers us, and to make a personal choice to seek (or not seek) the goal. Then we can become unfrozen in our pursuit.

Peak performance involves personal goals that are different from everyday achievements. We have to assume that our capabilities and achievements are far from ordinary. One way to cultivate a sense of vision about our goals and ideals is to think about other people who embody the highest ideals of what we would like to achieve. Their examples can guide us toward our own self-realization.

AWAKENING INTUITION

One of the key elements of peak performers is their creative problem solving. While rational and technological thinking emphasizes orderly paths and somewhat closed systems where we apply certain procedures to solve problems that have a single best solution, there are other ways of thinking and seeing the world. Clearly, for many types of work today, we must be familiar with technological systems of various sorts.

However, another type of thinking is essential to peak performance—the ability to come up with novel solutions, to discover new methods, to create the method that does what is needed in half the time or half the cost. While technical thinking follows established, linear pathways, creative thinking proceeds by leaps and unexpected, unpredictable alterations.

The study of creative and intuitive thought has recently been linked to psychophysiological findings about brain functioning. It seems that the two hemispheres of the brain operate according to different styles and modes. The left side of the brain, which is connected to the right side of the body, is responsible for linear, technical, and logical modes of thinking. It has its own characteristic brain-wave patterns and, in most people, is the dominant form of thought.

The right side of the brain seems to predominate and swing into operation when the person engages in artistic, metaphorical, or non-logical, intuitive thinking. For many of us such forms of thought have been de-emphasized in education and in work and we have lost touch with it. Right-brain thought has been linked with peak performance and creative thinking. It predominates during the flow state and at times when intuitive solutions to problems emerge.

Right-brain thought presents us with the unexpected and the unusual. It is fanciful, often humorous, and is not hampered by realistic notions of what can be done. When we place ourselves in the relaxation state, gently focus our attention on a problem or situation, and then simply observe and play with whatever images or scenes arise, we use the right side of our brain. Creative leaps often occur when an inventor is not consciously thinking of a problem. An image or thought comes to mind, perhaps seemingly unrelated. Then the person notes the implications of the thought and a sort of "aha!" experience takes place. This also takes place in dreams. Dreams and fantasies are very useful to peak performers. They are comfortable with the intuitive products of their minds.

But intuitive and creative work is not right-brain fantasy alone. Fantasy and creative imagery are common to everyone, but the images must be harnessed and connected to practical pursuits. The intuition must be reconnected and integrated with the left-brain systems of logical means to an end. Enhanced creativity must then be focused, and a good deal of work and energy must be applied to putting a new system into operation. There is a large gap between an image of a new product or system and its implementation. Both sides of the brain must be coordinated to create a peak performance.

Peak performers approach problems in a certain way that can be cultivated. Basically a problem or a demand is a pressure to perform. This creates tension. Certain types of tasks create more pressure, because the way to achieve success is vague or ambiguous. Many situations are unclear and we have to choose between alternatives with incomplete information. There is always an element of risk and uncertainty.

Peak performers can tolerate this tension without jumping to a quick solution or doing the usual thing. By carrying tension longer, and being comfortable with it, peak performers focus their intuitive and unconscious minds, along with their conscious technical ability, on the problem.

THE PEAK PERFORMANCE TEAM

We associate peak performance with individual achievement, heroism, and isolation—the astronaut, Olympic competitor, artist, or industrial magnate. Yet most peak performances are not solo efforts. Behind most achievements is a team of people who share the concentration, dedication, and creative pursuit of the goal. Or more commonly, peak performance is inspired by a group or organization that cares for the individual and demands the best.

Peak performers in organizations often note that they improved their performance because they felt that their co-workers, or organization, believed in them. They responded in kind to the positive expectations. In other situations the organization's mission or goal is so important to the individual that it empowers him or her to achieve. Or a work group may care for or respect each other to the degree that they cooperatively achieve peak performances.

In peak performing groups there is sharing of information, teamwork, and a high level of trust and caring. When these qualities are increased in work groups, as suggested earlier, the health, well-being, and performance level of individuals increase.

Peak Organizations

When you began this book, you probably held the popular notion that burnout, stress management, and personal effectiveness are qualities that belong to individuals. If you had a healthy personality, the benefits of education, and natural skills, you would be good at managing stress and move away from burning out in the direction of peak performance.

Yet most of us maintain a funny contradiction in our thoughts. In addition to placing the responsibility for stress management and peak performance on the individual, we tend to see stress and pressure as external forces that we are often powerless to prevent or respond to effectively. We simultaneously make ourselves responsible for our performance, and see ourselves as powerless before the forces of stress and pressure.

This workbook has tried to break down this confusion into elements that we can understand and master. The theme is that burnout and peak performance are things that we *can* influence. We can learn the skills to move us from burnout, through our daily pressures and stresses, toward peak performance.

However, as we reach the end of this journey, we come to another level and another way of looking at the whole area of performance. As we have seen, everything—from stress to health to well-being to peak performance—depends not only on individual skill and efficacy, but on qualities of the work group, the environment, and the organization.

The past two years have seen the birth of a new notion—or the resurgence of an old one—that the health, well-being, and effectiveness of an individual are critically affected by the organization and the environment in which he or she works. It is difficult for an energetic and dedicated individual to avoid burnout and to excel in an organization that creates stress.

Thus the focus of the search for balance is shifting from the individual to environments, organizations, and contexts that promote these qualities. That does not devalue the role of personal power in creating change, because it is indeed visionary and peak-performing individuals who have to work together to create the peak-performing organizations.

It is exciting to discover that the same qualities of empowerment, self-awareness, self-management, self-renewal, and peak performance that characterize individual health can also be applied to organizations. Each quality and exercise that can be used by an individual or a work group can also be applied, with only a little adjustment, to an organization. Like a person, an organization, a family, or a community is an organism that copes with pressure, adapts to change, and maintains itself. It can do so in a healthy, adaptive way, or in a dysfunctional way. As organizations extend their search for personal excellence and well-being, they will begin to see themselves as an organism needing awareness, competence, power, and nurture to survive and thrive.

References

Benson, Herbert. *The Relaxation Response*. New York: Morrow, 1975.

Benson, Herbert, and Robert L. Allen. "How Much Stress Is Too Much?" *Harvard Business Review*, September 1980.

Burns, David. *Feeling Good: The New Mood Therapy*. New York: Morrow, 1980.

Czikszentmihalyi, Mihaly. *Beyond Boredom and Anxiety*. San Francisco: Jossey-Bass, 1975.

Freudenberger, Herbert, and G. Richelson. *Burnout: The High Cost of High Achievement*. New York: Bantam, 1980.

Friedman, Meyer, and Ray Rosenman. *Type A Behavior and Your Heart*. New York: Fawcett, 1974.

Garfield, Charles. "Peak Performance." Lecture at Saybrook Institute, 1983.

Healthy People. U.S. Dept. HHS Monograph #79-55071. 1979.

Jaffe, Dennis. *Healing from Within*. New York: Bantam, 1983.

Kiev, Ari. *Executive Stress*. New York: AMACON, 1980.

Knowles, John, ed. *Doing Better and Feeling Worse*. New York: Norton, 1978.

Kobasa, Suzanne. "Stressful Life Events, Personality and Health," *Journal of Personality and Social Psychology* 37 (1979).

Lakein, Alan. *How to Get Control of Your Time and Your Life*. New York: Signet, 1973.

Lazarus, Richard. "Hassles of Life." *Psychology Today*, March 1981.

Lifton, Robert J. *The Broken Connection*. New York: Simon and Schuster, 1979.

Maslow, Abraham. *Toward a Psychology of Being*. Second Edition. New York: Van Nostrand, 1973.

Ogilvy, Jay. *Many-Dimensional Man*. New York: Harper & Row, 1981.

Pelletier, Kenneth. *Mind as Healer, Mind as Slayer*. New York: Delta, 1977.

Pines, Ayala, Eliot Aronson and Ditsa Kafry. *Burnout*. New York: Free Press, 1981.

Rahe, Richard. "Life Events, Stress and Health." Lecture at UCLA School of Medicine, November 1980.

Rubin, Lillian. *Intimate Strangers*. New York: Harper & Row, 1983.

Selye, Hans. *The Stress of Life*. New York: McGraw-Hill, 1976.

Toffler, Alvin. *Future Shock*. New York: Random House, 1976.

Travis, John, and Regina Ryan. *Wellness Workbook*. San Francisco: Ten Speed Press, 1981.

Resources

If you would like to have help in creating a burnout, stress management, health promotion, or peak performance program at your place of work, or if you would like help in creating your own personal program, here are some resources to help you.

American Association of Fitness Directors in Business and Industry:
  400 Sixth St. SW, Washington, DC 20201.
  A membership organization of health promotion and stress, management practitioners.

Center for Health Promotion and Education:
  Centers for Disease Control, Atlanta, GA 30333. 404-329-3235.
  Provides technical assistance, publishes research, and helps in creating stress and health programs, and disseminates a large number of monographs.

Essi Systems:
  764A Ashbury St, San Francisco, CA 94117. 415-665-8699. Cynthia Scott, Dennis Jaffe, and Esther Orioli.
  A resource center helping organizations and health clinics create stress and personal performance programs. Publishes *Personal Stress Inventory*, tapes and other training materials.

Execu-Fit Health Programs:
  3580 California Street, Suite 304, San Francisco, CA 94118. 415-929-9407. Karen Behnke.
  Creates health and stress programs for companies, and provides health resources and seminars on-site.

Medical Self-Care:
  P.O. Box 717, Inverness, CA 94937. Tom Ferguson.
  National magazine of current information about health promotion and self-care.

Source.—Software for the Mind:
  P.O. Box W, Stanford, CA 94305. Emmett Miller.
  Complete line of cassettes and other learning materials for health and stress programs.

Washington Business Group on Health:
  922 Pennsylvania Ave. SE, Washington, DC 20003. 202-547-6644. Willis Goldbeck.
  A national organization of corporations that provides resources and information about health promotion. Publishes magazine *Work and Health*.

INDEX

A

B

Y

ABOUT THE AUTHORS

Dennis T. Jaffe, Ph.D., and Cynthia D. Scott, Ph.D., are clinical psychologists and management consultants who are concerned with the personal development of people who work within organizations and health-care settings, and the impact of their growth on the effectiveness of the work setting. They have worked with scores of organizations over the past ten years, lecturing, conducting seminars, and helping work groups function more effectively.

They work through Performance Designs, at 764 Ashbury Street, San Francisco, CA 94117, and Learning for Health, at 1314 Westwood Boulevard, Los Angeles, CA 90024. In addition to seminars and consultation, they offer a variety of educational materials, including a *Personal Stress Inventory*, containing many of the self-assessment instruments abstracted in this book, and cassette tapes containing many of the exercises reprinted here, at greater length. Write them for further information.

Dennis T. Jaffe received an M.A. degree in management and a Ph.D. in sociology from Yale University, and is Associate Professor of Psychology and co-director of the Health Studies program at Saybrook Institute, San Francisco. He is currently president of the Association for Humanistic Psychology, and is author of *Healing from Within* (winner of the 1980 Medical Self-Care Book Award), *Body, Mind and Health,* and several professional textbooks. Cynthia D. Scott, M.P.H., Ph.D., is a member of the clinical faculty of the University of California San Francisco School of Medicine, and co-editor of *Eldercare,* and *Heal Thyself: The Health of Health Professionals.*

5 425246

Catalog

If you are interested in a list of fine Paperback
books, covering a wide range of subjects
and interests, send your name and address,
requesting your free catalog, to:

McGraw-Hill Paperbacks
1221 Avenue of Americas
New York, N.Y. 10020

5 425246

A